ISLAMICIZING AMERICA

Imam Abdallah Yasin

TO SOW THE FALLOW SOIL

James C. Winston
Publishing Company, Inc.
Trade Division of Winston-Derek Publishers Group, Inc.

First printing 1996

Back cover quotes from *Prophecies of the Holy Qur'an* by `Ali Akbar.
Inside front cover quote from *Veiled Mysteries of Egypt.*
Inside back cover quote from Rev. Taylor's lecture on "Mahomedanism", Church Congress at Wolverhampton, October 7, 1887.

PUBLISHED BY JAMES C. WINSTON PUBLISHING COMPANY, INC.
Nashville, Tennessee 37205

Library of Congress Catalog Card No: 94-61159
ISBN: 1-55523-724-X

Printed in the United States of America

TO THE MEMORY OF MY PARENTS

"Lord, have your mercy upon them
just as they brought me up with kindness
and affection when I was little."

Qur'aan 17:24

TABLE OF CONTENTS

PREFACE

This book is the compilation of
a series of articles published in the Islamic
publication *Shahadah*,
as prefaced below.

"Because of Prevailing Issues in the Islamic
Community At-Large, the Editorial Staff of
Shahadah saw the need for these issues to be
addressed by Imam Abdallah Yasin, Amir of
The International Islamic Community Of Masjid
Baytul-Khaliq, Inc. In each issue of *Shahadah*
the ES intends to present a particular
prevailing issue. Insha'Allah."

INTRODUCTION

Herein are a collection of interviews with Imam Abdallah Yasin on many critical subjects concerning American Society at-large. These interviews were previously published in the *Shahadah Journal* which is the official organ of the International Islamic Community Of Masjid Baytul-Khaliq, Inc. of which Imam Abdallah is and has been the Amir for the past twenty-three years.

Herein, Imam Abdallah attempts, by suggestion, with Orthodox Islamic insight and by design, to depict that Islam has the answers which today's Society is seeking to combat her many moral and social ills.

Through his presentations we gain an acute and valuable inside look at the general mind-set of one of America's fastest growing, most peaceful and law abiding citizen groups (Orthodox Muslims), which is striving to become an indelible part of the American scene.

The Editorial Staff of *Shahadah*, 1995
Shaykh Abdur-Rashid IsHaq
Shaykh Saleem MuHammad

ABOUT THE AUTHOR

Imam Abdallah Yasin, the Amir (Overall Organization Leader) of the New Jersey-based Islamic Community/ Congregation of Masjid Baytul-Khaliq for twenty-three years, is well known nationally and abroad for his Islamic work and contributions. He is a principal Islamic leader in the Virgin Islands, preaches at the local mosque and administers to his national organizational affairs. Until his 1988 relocation to St. Croix, he was Imam at Newark's Community Mosque; was a founder and first Chairman of the Islamic Council of Essex County and also of the Unified Eid Committee of New Jersey. He was a founder of the North American Islamic Federation and its national treasurer; hosted "Islamic Discussions", a popular New Jersey cable program. For twelve years, he was a dedicated member of Saudi Arabia's United States Islamic Propagation Team. He is currently the Secretary-General of The Council of Imams of New Jersey and the Director of the Da'wah Center of the U.S. Virgin Islands. He is affiliated with several National Organizations and represents his organization internationally through the Council of Mosques of the United States and Canada.

Imam Abdallah is a past board member of St. Croix's Interfaith Coalition. He has just finished two years hosting "Islamic Perspectives", a popular radio program broadcasting to the Caribbean. Imam Abdallah's formal schooling took place in New Jersey and New York. He has successfully completed courses of study at several Islamic institutions of higher learning in the United States and abroad. After 25 years he is retired from the engineering profession, is married and has seven children, ages 32 to 12.

CHAPTER 1
HOW DO WE GET THERE FROM HERE?

ES: Imam Abdallah, As-salaamu 'alaykum.

Imam: Wa-'alaykumus-salaam wa raHmatullah.

ES: Imam Abdallah, based upon some of our in-house discussions, we present the following question/idea as a general concern of Muslims.Though we call it a general concern, to our know-ledge, it has not been publicly addressed, although the time is certainly at hand. First let us qualify what will follow by quoting All-Mighty Allah:

"He it is Who has sent His Apostle with the Guidance and the Religion of Truth (wa deenil-Haqq) that He may cause it to prevail over all religion, even though the Polytheists (the Pagans) may detest (it)." Qur'aan 61:9 (Also see 9:33 and 48:28)

Qur'aanic interpreter Shaykh Abdullah Yusuf Ali's note to this verse states: "Over all religion: in the singular: not over all religions, in the plural. There is really only one true religion, The Message of God, submission to the will of God: this is called Islam. It was the religion preached by Moses and Jesus; it was the religion of Abraham, Noah and all the prophets, by whatever name it may be called. If people corrupt the pure light, and call their religions by different names, we must bear with them, and we may allow the names for convenience. But Truth must prevail over all."[1]

Now our question/idea. We would like for you to open the door to intelligent conjecture. How is it possible for Muslims to help Allah'sTruth to prevail in America? What direction, means, opportunities, avenues, etc., are to be used to bring about this effect? In other words: please give our readers an intellectual perspective of "How do we get there from here?" in regard to Islamicizing America.

Imam Abdallah:

This is not a matter to be answered hurriedly. However, Allah (The Glorious and The Most High) tells us that man plans and Allah plans and that He, Allah, is The Best of Planners. Does this mean that man should not plan; that he should do nothing and leave everything in Allah's hands? NO! Simply put, what this means is that man should strive to achieve his goals while acknowledging that it is Allah Who is really in control. With this logic, man can accept his fate, good or bad, with a constant outlook of Hope.

What is attempted (Insha'Allah) to be presented in these pages and those which follow is not meant to be a blueprint nor the plan for bringing about change. What follows is an attempt to begin an intellectually realistic and practical dialogue on this critical subject.

First of all let us clear up a major point. To bring this about, the Islamicizing of the U. S. of A. will necessitate millions of Great Jihads. Allah, the Sovereign of The Universe, says: ".......Verily never will Allah change the condition of a people until they change it themselves (with their own souls)."   Qur'aan 13:11 These jihads are the individual jihads (struggles) by each of the millions of Muslims in this country to act Islamically, by correcting the errors of their own personal, private and public lives, as best they can.

This will not happen en masse until they begin, en masse, to accept Islamic Leadership which is based only upon the Qur'aan and the Sunnah. Once this begins to happen, and I sincerely believe it will, we will find Americans

2

accepting Islam from quarters we had not expected. Those 'existing' individual local and national groups of Muslims will all but pale into insignificance by the overwhelming numbers of prospective Muslims in American society who are only a hands breadth away from accepting Islam. Insha'Allah.

.I do not see armed struggle nor violence in bringing about this national change. If there is an armed struggle on our part, it will only happen as a survival and defensive measure. We will not be armed aggressors. The unfortunate racial rebellions we have witnessed in this country over the past several decades are not a part of Islamic history here in America.

However, on that point let it be said to all, that were the rank and file of oppressed people in America Muslims, they would not be in the deplorable condition they are in. Further, Islam is their only way out! All-Mighty Allah says: "Tumult and oppression are worse than slaughter" Qur'aan 2:191, 217.

When I stated above that I do not envision violence to effect this change, I do not state this out of fear, on the contrary, but out of reason. The only One to be feared is Allah. Not only has He caused planets and solar systems to cease to exist, He can, without effort, humble any nation on earth as He has already done numerous times in man's history by natural means. Allah can cause the Earth to open and swallow any armed man or nation along with its weapons of war. Man and his missiles are no match for Allah's wrath. Man should take heed, for as I pen these very words Hurricane Andrew is pounding Florida and there is nothing man can do to prevent its destruction! Nothing!

Not fear, but reason. This is a 'modern' age and only an absolute fool would endeavor to return man to the Dark Ages by violence. As a point of fact, the scientific and technological advances of the West are based heavily upon

3

the incredible achievements during the Eight Hundred years rule by the Moors of Andalus (Spain and Portugal). Europeans did all they could to eliminate the racial identity of these Moors and deny them their place in history. And when Europe traces its roots of civilization to Greece (Aristotle, Plato, Pythagoras, etcetera), examination of the facts will prove once again that Africans (principally from Egypt and Nubia) were their teachers.

It should be noted that during the Persian, Greek and Roman invasions of Egypt, many of the learned men (priests, teachers, etc.) escaped these invaders by fleeing into the neighboring states of North Africa, carrying their treasures of learning, knowledge and wisdom with them. In truth, their learning was the foundation upon which the Moors built their civilization once in al-Andalusia! Therefore, in reality the achievements of the human race, from sub-marines to spacecraft, from television to computors, from lasers to medicine, are as much the glory of the African race as of the European. So why destroy them?

Mamadou Chinyelu in his treatise, AFRICANS AND THE BIRTH AND EXPANSION OF ISLAM, says: "Though the Moors lost military, political and economic control of Spain, their influence lingered long after their physical departure. Spain and Portugal, more than any other European populations, derived enormous benefits from the Moorish and African Muslim presence. They became, for awhile, world leaders in the nautical sciences. And, it was not until 1588 (with the defeat of the Spanish Armada) that the other European nations were able to challenge them and become serious rivals in the game of discovery and colonization.

With Spain and Portugal in the lead, Europe as a whole profited enormously from Moorish civilization. Jackson quotes a historian assaying that, "None of our modern sophistry redeems the squalor of Europe from the fifth to the eleventh century." [2] Stanley Lane-Poole provides us with a most vivid description of the contrast between Moorish Spain and the backwardness of the other European countries:

Cordova was the wonderful city of the tenth century; the streets were well paved and there were raised sidewalks for pedestrians. At night one could walk for ten miles by the light of lamps, flanked by an uninterrupted extent of buildings. All this was hundreds of years before there was a paved street in Paris or a street lamp in London. Cordova with a population exceeding one million was served by four thousand public markets and five thousand mills. Its public baths numbered into the hundreds, when bathing in the rest of Europe was frowned upon as a diabolical custom, avoided by good Christians. Moorish monarchs dwelt in sumptuous palaces, while the crowned heads of England, France and Germany lived in big barns, lacking both windows and chimneys and with only a hole in the roof for the exit of smoke.

Education was universal in Moslem Spain, being given to the most humble, while in Christian Europe 99 percent of the populace was illiterate, and even kings could neither read nor write. In the tenth and eleventh centuries, public libraries in Spain could boast of more than seventy, of which the one in Cordova housed 600,000 manuscripts. Christian Europe contained only two universities of any consequence, while in Spain there were seventeen outstanding universities. The finest were those located in Almeria, Cordova, Granada, Jaen, Malaga, Seville and Toledo. Scientific progress in astronomy, chemistry, physics, mathematics, geography and philology in Moslem Spain reached a high level of

development.   Scholars and artists formed associations to promote their particular studies, and scientific
congresses were organized to promote research and
facilitate the spread of knowledge.

The legacy of the Moors and the African Muslims
to European civilization has been largely ignored, hid-
den or denied and those who would expose the truth of
Europe's indebtedness to the Moors have been overlooked or locked away from mainstream information
sources. Yet, even a cursory review of Europe prior to
the Moorish presence, provides ample evidence of their
stumbling around in disorder and darkness. There can
be no doubt that the explorations of new worlds and
scientific, social, political and even public health and
urban developments would not have been possible
without their longstanding and fundamental contacts
with Moorish civilization." (See GOLDEN AGE OF THE
MOOR, edited by Ivan Van Sertima, pp. 377 -378) [3]

The foregoing was presented because black people
of African extraction who for the most part do not know nor
really believe in "their" achievements and accomplishments,
need to see the Moors in their greatness from fairly recent
days, historically speaking. Then, they will not disassociate
themselves from the higher sciences. Americans of African
descent tend to display a non-intellectual, non-contributory
attitude to society in the way of science and technology,
medicine, space technology, rockets, machines of transport-
sation and war, etc. The fact is that there are millions of
descendants of the above described Moors (Africans) in the
United States of America! Who came as free men!

When we speak of Islamicizing a society, we must
necessarily mean changing the direction of its culture. Must
everything be done away with? No! Only those aspects
which work against one's God-consciousness.

Must we convert the entire population of America to be successful? No! The example of Moorish Spain is ample example of religious tolerance and co-existence!

Allah (The Soveriegn of the Universe) says: "You are the best of Peoples, evolved for mankind, enjoining what is right, forbidding what is wrong, and believing in Allah. If only the People of the Book (Christians and Jews) had faith, it would be best for them: among them are some who have faith, but most of them are perverted transgressors." Qur'aan 3:100

The U.S. sorely needs the medicinal effects of Islam to save it from its disease of self-destruction. Her ideals are lofty but she does not have the moral strength to attain her ideals which can only become attainable with a notable Islamic presence and influence. Many Americans already share Islamic concerns in their hearts on such matters as abortion, homosexuality, drinking, gambling, etc.

For those who will use the argument of discrimination against certain groups, we can only relate the following. All-Mighty Allah says about the latter two: "They ask you concerning wine and gambling. Say: In them is great sin and some profit for men; but the sin is greater than the profit." Qur'aan 2:219

Yes! Sometimes the society must close certain doors (gambling, drinking, abortion, homosexuality, lewdness in the public media, etc.).This is not discrimination, this is about 'wisdom' that society utilizes this authority to protect itself.

Unlimited freedom is destructive. Just look at American (Western) women. Trying to be men! Abandoning their God-given role of the mothers of society. These so-called liberated women are not fighting against men, they are rebelling against God and challenging His authority to create! I agree that an unusually gifted woman should be allowed to fulfill her destiny with her God-given high intelligence even if it be outside her home and family. But this should be the exception, not the rule. Women abandoning the home is the first germ in the disease of family disintegration. This trend must be turned around. Although, if observed closely, one will find perverted men behind the scenes encouraging these wayward women on.

There are only two genders on the planet: male and female. And, whether one likes it or not, this is a man's world. And men are not going to be controlled by women, and her role as a woman does not entitle her to a fifty per-cent share in universal sovereignty. Her soul is equal to man's, but her role is not! Allah, The Glorious and The Most High, says: "Their Lord answers them saying: `I will deny no man or woman among you the reward of their labors. You are the offspring of one another.'" Q3:195 Also: ".....And women shall have rights similar to the rights against them, according to what is equitable; but men have a degree (of advantage) over them. And Allah is Exalted in power, Wise." Qur'aan 2:228 Also:"Men have authority over women because Allah has made the one superior to the other, and because they spend of their wealth to maintain them." Q4:34

If there is no turn around in this 'unisex attitude', it is the opinion of this writer that women in western countries will in time find themselves under a yoke of oppression by men unheard of in recent times. Islam is their salvation. Islam frees women, it does not enslave them as is widely misconceived by these same men! We are witnessing this female oppression growing today by leaps and bounds with women being raped and brutalized in record numbers. Why? With women and men so freely engaging in sex all around, just giving sex away; why the raping? This is male anger being expressed by weak men who are striking out at women for a variety of non-sexual reasons! Oppression!

Our primary effort boils down to giving good da`wah (invitation to Islam based upon good Muslim examples). When non-Muslim people look at a Muslim they see some-one who has wilfully given up (sacrificed) much of the social affiliations and contacts of this society. They see someone who is not a part of their setting. Someone who is different by what he/she believes concerning God. His/her family ties are intact though stretched and possibly strained. His per-sonal and moral values are filtered through his/her religion which removes much of what they accept as natural and normal.

However, what they must begin to see is how Islam has benefited that person. If what they see looks benefiting, interesting and attractive, only then will they begin to mental-ly explore the possibilities of themselves accepting Islam.

We shall be discussing ideas on Islamicizing America concerning such diverse topics as: entertainment and music, television, economics, religion, politics, industry, city/state communities, government, etc. Insha'Allah. We shall explore the impact of these American institutions on American and world society and how, why and what course of change is needed to make America the model society she dreams of being. Insha'Allah.

CHAPTER 2
CULTURE, NEIGHBORHOODS, SCHOOLS AND BUSINESSES

ES: Imam Abdallah, As-salaamu 'alaykum.

Imam: Wa-'alaykumus-salaam wa rahmatullah.

ES: Imam Abdallah, in our last issue of *Shahadah*, you began to explore a possibility and/or perhaps a methodology for Islamicizing America. We have received many interesting comments on your theme. Many Muslins have commented on not having previously taken a serious view on this matter and your article opened their eyes to a new Islamic dimension. We are happy to say that many are anticipating the continuation of this particular series.

Imam: Al-Hamdu lilaah. In the previous issue of *Shahadah*, among the things mentioned were how important it is for every Muslim man and woman to Islamically upgrade their own lives and the importance of accepting leadership.

What is the primary role of this leadership? It must be capable of organizing a body of people and lead them to be independent controllers of their own destiny. Let us explore:

First, I must make it absolutely clear that the design-plan(s) I present are geared primarily, though not exclusively, toward the African-American in general and African-American Muslim in particular. We dark-skinned, born-here Americans have to begin to look honestly at our selves and dutifully allow our leadership to determine what is our primary problem. We cannot at this time be overly concerned with our foreign-born brother who comes here and by and large makes our job more difficult by his disappointing Islamic posture. We must begin to effect our own agenda. One must be able to help himself before he is able to help anyone else.

What is the Problem!... Clearly, IT MUST BE the African-American's WAY OF LIFE! How he lives!

What is the answer?... The Answer is Islam.

Why Islam? ......Because the African-American is in search of an identity. Self Ignorance is worse today than it was thirty years ago! He seeks his true self, in which he believes and feels a comfortable connection to his past lineage, ancestral lives and common experiences. He needs the remembrance and reconnecting of a unifying experience to over-ride the nightmare of American Slavery which still predominates his thoughts and actions.

He seeks a CULTURE. He seeks his true cultural identity. Culture is the magnet which attracts and the glue which holds any ethnic community together. Today, we discuss CULTURE (which produces) "Neighborhoods" (which necessitate) "Islamic Schools" and Muslim owned and operated businesses.

The African-American knows that he is somebody! But who? Christianity has not taught him. For a time, it was a safety-line to help him until he "learned how to swim, got on his own two feet, learned to think for himself". Christianity was never intended to help him gain his freedom! He was not Christian when he came here! Can not today's African-American leadership see that this "religion" was only meant to be temporarily used as a surreptitious "survival tool"? Certainly his leadership can see that for the past two centuries it has all but failed him and the rest of the world? Can not his leadership see that the Pauline Christians of today are not the early Christians, who, though they were Jews, were in fact the Muslims of their time?

Of course they can.... They don't want to! Evidently their present standings, in their minds, would be jeopardized.

When speaking of religions, it should be emphasized that Islam is not a religion! Islam is a "way of life" and we must always look upon it as such. From this day on, we should never again refer to Islam as a religion. Religion is the wanderings of man's mind. As my esteemed brother Shaykh Ibrahim Isma`il used to say, "Religion is man's preservation of his cultural/historical-relics which have little or no connection with God." (May Allah's Mercy be upon him)

The world over, man has allowed his natural way of life to become interrupted and diverted into something unnatural and mystical. Then, to explain what before had no need of explanation was born a needless plethora of religion along with man's wrongful domination of people through it; all the while saying that it is in the name of God.

Especially when talking to non-Muslims, Muslims must learn how to be non-religious. Our position should be a desire to live in harmony within God's universe. Always be very clear, frank and careful in making and accepting religious statements. As Muslims we do not have to accept any hocus-pocus. God Is One. No, He can't be seen. We know that God has revealed Himself to us and in so doing has made us Muslim. Al-Hamdulilaah! All the hocus-pocus must come from the side of confusion and uncertainty". That is one of the trappings of Christianity's "Trinity". Pagan belief. So, in dealing with the Islamic position on any matter we must always be straightforward and spiritually scientific. Science is continually verifying All-Mighty Allah's Book, Al-Qur'aanul-Kareem. No other book exists which is so True.

And I say this in all seriousness: the mind of the black Christian has been truly displaced, if in fact he really

13

believes in his doctrines of religion — anyone who really believes, in his/her heart and soul that God sent His son.......to be slaughtered ....on their behalf.....and after witnessing centuries of seeing his/her forefathers dying in similar manners by the hands of Christians only because they are black people! And God has sent His son, (nastagh-firullah) His only son, their savior!

Black people of America need to stop, wake up and face it — what good is a religion if it doesn't better your condition? These people have been duped concerning the very nature of God to even think that He would have a "son". This idea is pagan. Anyone can pray to God but the question is how does one pray so as to expect an eventual answer. Oftimes the heartfelt desire to be good Christians has gotten black Christians killed... by white Christians... with impunity.

Wake up Africans, this religion is killing you; worse, it is a tool of your continual enslavement. Unlike Islam, which assures you of success in this life as well as the hereafter, if this is what you strive for, Christianity promises no reward in this world, but that "pie in the sky." Christians are the one's making the news everyday. Just read the newspapers and watch T.V. This is the state of mind of religious people. Religion will make one believe the absurd rather than the obvious, all while they are being destroyed, at times by their own hands!

Praying to God is good because it directs one to what has to be done. But God won't do it for you. One makes the honest effort and God may lend a hand. "Because Allah will never change a favor which he has conferred upon a people until they change their own condition: And Allah is All Hearing, All Knowing." Qur'aan 8:53

Islam is not a religion, it is 'a way of life'. Just live life according to God's will as taught by His prophets; all of whom were Muslim.

Definition of Muslim: One who submits to Allah's will. Period. It is so simple. Islam has realistic parameters with realistic human role models. The most exemplary of whom is Prophet MuHammad (PBUH).

It is time for whole Christian congregations to be led as groups of people, by their respective leaders, into the reality of Islam and the UNION of Church and State rather than its separation. The controllers of the U. S. of A. have continually tricked the African-American by appealing to his weaknesses and his naffs (low desires). The enslaved black men and women who looked upon Christianity as their only means of survival became rutted into it and became utilized by their leadership as political pawns. African-American Christians out of dispair simply accepted Christianity as their lot while their leadership began to preach to them that their hopes of freedom now lie in the Political Arena!

Do not the African-American leadership know that no previously enslaved minority ever ever won their freedom through politics? They should by now! And what do most of these politicians have in common? That's right — religion. What else??? As free people, planners of their own destinies, they have independent cultures...... all except the African-American that is. The African-American is in a game of Religion and another of Politics. The deck is stacked against him on both fronts. But his blind faith keeps him going...... and his lack of intelligence* (this explained later).

Because of the nature of Politics, if it is not incorporated within the people's system of Faith, it will become Religion's companion-conspirator against the people who are caught between the two, not recognizing that both represent the seed, tree and the fruit of idol worship. This is because all religion is based upon false and/or man-corrupted evidence. God Is One. Faith in Him Is One. Service to Him Is One for ALL. When we look at all the religions of the world we see a mockery of God through people's misguided/misdirected God-consciousness.

Now before I go any further, the African-American is in limbo. We must attempt to wake him up by kind and intelligent conversation in which we casually or otherwise remind him that we don't relate to religion. We simply acknowledge God as He has designed for all men to do. The Christian must always be reminded that God is not 'in' His creation. Explain what 'shirk' is (ascribing partners to Allah), and ways to avoid it. Leave his world of religion and give him cause to think and perhaps, Insha'Allah, Allah will guide him to Islam. "For the worst of beasts in the sight of Allah are those who reject Him: They will not believe." Qur'aan 8:55

What is now being approached by the African-American is his final stage of self and group analysis and terminal re-identification. In this final re-examination and appraisal stage, he must find the courage to throw off all the religious and social trappings which have held him back in order that he might be capable of seeing the forest. He must make an honest assessment of himself, for himself. He need become a free thinker. Religion — not organization, but religion — must be abandoned. We realize the necessity of being organized in our existence and we can give thanks to the "Church" for that, alone. The necessity for structure is universal.

But it is past time for a new strategy, a new way of viewing life, new definitions. It is not ludicrous to expect entire Christian congregations to accept, practice and promote Islam. They must leave one "brotherhood" for another

16

which awaits them with open arms. These are very smart and able people who have been sidetracked. Islam will make them intelligent and put their intelligence to good use. Insha'Allah, for intelligence is the correct knowledge of God* (note statement earlier).

Therefore, we Muslims must be capable of seeing that African-Americans (including ourselves) are at the most critical point of our history on these shores relative to shaping our own destiny. Also, if we African-Americans know anything of history, we must know that other Africans came to these American shores whose blood runs in our veins. Recognizing this, our blood begins to be more culturally pronounced than the African ethnic-mix which slavery forced upon us and which heretofore was all we had to identify with. This was virtually unidentifiable other than the fact that we shared a common color and a common hatred by Europeans.

In the African-American's historical search he will find that great numbers of Arab-Moors (Hamitic-Arabs), whose skin was the color of rich soil, had come to America, some much earlier, but mainly with the fall of Muslim Spain in 1492. The Moors brought an intact culture though they abandoned their Islam. When they did so, rips and tears began to destroy the fabric of their culture and they seemingly disappeared from the American scene. Seemingly.

This teaches us an important lesson. Islam IS the answer. Without it, for us, even a culture cannot survive. However, there is an old saying that one should be careful how one treats people on the way up because one meets the same people on the way down. This is precisely true with values, concepts and stages of man's upward striving. In returning home from being lost, it is wise to return by the route one came. We must become re-culturalized. Culture binds a people. Lose it and the loss of its people is not far behind.

Some might say that Islam is our culture. To that I say this: Islam is the genesis of the cultures of all non-religious peoples who acknowledge the existence of Allah. To ignore the individualic reality of the various cultures of Islamic Peoples is not real. Islam is the basic format for the development of our specific cultures; however, a group's culture develops as an outward and inward expression of their free application of self-determination.

CULTURE is the magnet which attracts and the glue which binds people together. Unfortunately, in his desperate search for his "true identity", his "true self", the African-American in looking back to Africa has adopted pagan replacements for what is ailing him and they in turn, fail him. He must stop overlooking the fact that Africa's greatest moments were under the banner of Islam.....That Islam is more of an African 'way of life' than it is Asian..... That without the aid of Africans Islam would have been stymied in Arabia....That the Muslims had a very difficult time conquering Africans and only by the Grace of All-Mighty Allah did a number of key African rulers accept Islam and brought their people over.

What is more of a glaring statement of the failure of these people who refuse to honestly see Islam, than to watch a choir of Christian African-Americans, many of whom are dressed in quasi African garb, singing Christian spirituals? Their 'going back to Africa' was only to find new 'rags' to wear on Sunday, not to change their thought patterns which are more in need of changing than their clothing. African-Americans, including Muslims, need reculturalizing.

ES: Imam Abdallah, as you well know, it is our hope and our task for the *Shahadah Educational Journal* to stimulate thought and certainly your thought on these matters is provocative. It is also well known that the leadership of Masjid Baytul-Khaliq has long endorsed the idea that Muslims should live in one locality in any City in which they exist in significant numbers. For over a decade this call has received no sanction by local leadership. At the outset you stated that today's agenda would include "Neighborhoods" and "Islamic Schools" and Muslim owned and operated businesses", so perhaps we are being presented this list as per their order of importance?

Imam: Yes. Exactly. Commonality is the one and only factor which groups people together in a manner which somehow takes the decision out of their hands! A common culture or 'acknowledgement' of a common culture automatically forms a neighborhood. We have not as yet acknowledged this commonality! The proof of this statement is that we have virtually no African-American Muslim neighborhoods to speak of! Oh yes, there are plenty of African-American neighborhoods all over the country. They exist by the plan of 'profiteering' Judeo/Christians, not by the choice of the African-Americans who reside in them.

In the Muslim's case, the leadership need be courageous and smart enough to direct their people where to live. As has been said before by us, the leaders need to group and accept leadership among themselves from themselves over themselves. But they too are without a 'cultural acknowledgement' and therefore have been stymied on how to effect this without becoming unpopular. This must eventually be accomplished and can only sensibly and peacefully be accomplished and maintained through a collective leadership decision, especially in large cities.

This would be an act of choice. An act of "free men" taking a hand in shaping their own destiny and that of their progeny. Formation of our own Muslim neighborhoods would begin to cure many of today's social ills which afflict us. We would be governing ourselves primarily by simple casual everyday obsevation of each other as neighbors and the willingness to insist upon and enforce 'right public conduct' by the community leader(s), the 'governing authority'.

The importance of living among each other cannot be over emphasized. It is an imposed duty. Imaam MuHyuddeen Ibn Sharaf an-Nawaweyy (d. 676/1277) cites in his book of fiqh (law), al-Majmuu` Sharh al-Muhadhdhab. It was recorded by At-Tirmidhee, Abu Daa`uud, An--Naaa`ee and Ibn Maajah from Jareer Ibn Abdullah (may Allah be pleased with them all) that: The Messenger of Allah (PBUH) sent troops to Khath`am (a tribe near Ta`if). People sought refuge by prostrating, but they were rapidly killed. This news reached the Prophet (PBUH), so he ordered one half the usual amount of 'blood money' be paid for them and he said: "I am not responsible for any Muslim who lives among the polytheist." The Companions said: "O Messenger of Allah (PBUH)! Why?" He replied: "You are not able to see each other's fire (home).

This hadeeth directly relates to Muslims living among non-Muslims. In this hadeeth the Prophet (PBUH) regards Muslims living close to each other as neighbors to be a matter of life and death. Muslims were ordered to form neighborhoods in order that they might distinguish themselves from non-Muslims and be recognized by others. If Muslims were not collectively recognizable as Muslims, then the Prophet (PBUH) could not hold other Muslims responsible for mistaking them for non-Muslims.

Here is another statement from the Prophet (PBUH) which sheds more light on why he was so strong on the concern of Muslims living in non-Muslim countries to form Muslim neighborhoods. MuHammad Ibn `Abdul-WaaHid, (d.483/1090), in his book of fiqh, Shar Fath al-Qadeer, reports: The Messenger Of Allah (PBUH) ruled that "if a Muslim is killed among the ranks of non-believers, blood money is not required because his protection is elimianted by the largeness of their numbers." He also said: "Whoever increases the largeness of the numbers of a people, he is one of them."

These hadeeth advocate Muslims being separate from non-Muslims in locality and identity. Another hadeeth which is similar to the above is more direct in discouraging Muslims from intermingling with non-Muslims. Abu Daa`uud and At-Tirmedhee recorded that Samurah Ibn Jundub narrated that the Prophet (PBUH) said: "Do not live among polytheists and do not join them." This hadeeth is said to be "hasan" (good).

The essence of the Prophet's (PBUH) thinking appears to be that living amongst a people can lead to association, association as a minority can lead to assimilation, and assimilation with non-Muslims must be avoided.Forming neighborhoods would not only move to purify our ranks but would increase our numbers because non-Muslims would want to live among us as as well as attend our schools as a means of escaping the crime of other areas! They and their children would be exposed to our cultural values and possibly affected. The effect upon them should prove to be even more pronounced than their present affect and effect upon us now as we live among them... a condition for change which must take priority.

We must be willing to be governed Islamically. Why do I say governed? Because your neighborhood is your first and primary land base. Every independent people have a land base. So consider how far we are from being free and independent and we don't even have a neighborhood!

Although there are democratic avenues and procedures allowed and used in Islamic government, that government is not a Democracy. Islam has never given sanction to a country-wide, one man—one vote concept. It does not promote a democratic society per se. In the development of our Muslim neighborhoods it is well that we acknowledge the following: A democratic society always reflects its ills publically. A society which legalizes drugs (alchohol, the worst drug of all), is necessarily going to act belligerently and act hypocritically. People get government they deserve.

On the other hand Islam does not allow that every lying, scandalous, adulterous, foolish, whore-mongering, cheating, uncouth, known dishonest, imbibing or any sinner to have a say in governing society, nor your neighborhoods, nor your communities! Western styled Judeo/Christian society does. LOOK AT IT. America! Barely two hundred years old and it is in a state of decadence! Civilized Europe is little older and is close on her heels.

As Islam, through the Moors, provided the light by which Europe came out of her darkness, so it can be for Muslims (Moors?) to give light for America to come out of her darkness. Insha'Allah. We must discourage crime by Islamically developing and personalizing our neighborhoods to the detriment of any unlawful outside influences. We should want our police to stop any group of youths who are out past a certain time. Our police MUST always be most polite, courteous and helpful.

All concerned neighorhoods (communities) must use all available righteous means to prohibit after dark carousing within their respective areas. This is called maintaining the Peace. Our Prophet (PBUH) is reported to have said: "When it becomes dark gather yourself and your family indoors." In Muslim neighborhoods, Islamic law must prevail as far as the Leadership or governing body determines. Anyone who says you can't practice Islamic Law among Muslims anywhere is walking backwards with his eyes closed. Or is a foreigner and doesn't know what the heck it is like to live in America.

Islamic Law is exemplary. Without it, the Law, there is no Islamic Society, in your nerighborhoods or anywhere. There would be no restraint upon those Muslims and others who would bring the filth of the greater society into the midst of your Muslim community/neighborhood. Only the criminal fears The Law.

Islamic law would only supplement 'the law of the land' and would only supercede it if and when Islamic Dictates demanded. This is not vigilanteism; it is 'righteous' control of our neighborhoods, where we would live and bring up our families. This control is not based upon race, creed, color nor religion but upon the Law of Allah and the Sunnah of His Messenger (PBUH) to treat every human with respect and revere all life which is beyond our ability to create.

This example would induce other communities to do the same throughout America! Bringing in a "new" age of God-consciousness. Bringing in a "new" America. There must be a new America as the old and present America is in a state of downward spiraling grid-lock. We must be willing to use The Law to keep people who are inclined to wrong-doing, in check. That's what it is for!

Today, one finds all sorts of un-changed people trying to save their children. When will they realize that if they can't change/save themselves, they can't save anyone? What good is it to educate Muslim children in an Islamic setting and then send them off into the world baseless? With no "land base" for them to relate to, to help develop, to return to? They are sent off to pagan colleges which in turn work overtime to remove God from their consciousness.

How many times have we, in blessed ignorance, marvelled at our babies dressed up to look like adult Muslims, going to an "Islamic School"? How many schools start off at kindergarten, first and second grade with the intent to add a grade each year? Many. Too many. Why not start at high school? After all, junior high and high school age is when and where we are losing our children. The younger children would benefit just as well being taught at home or in weekend schools.

Also, our outlook is different from that of the main society, by who we are and our collective experiences, racialy and psycologically. We cannot continue to pattern our Muslim schools after the non-Muslim. We come up learning from an educational pattern which is not only uninteresting but oftimes dis-interesting as well to many of our children. The attitude and needs of the Established Neighborhood and the aspirations of its people is what shapes the development of its school system.

The majority of our past and present leadership must bear the weight for the futility of the above scenario. Why? Because we all have to live somewhere. Why not live together and by weight of numbers Muslims would eventually control the public school(s) in their neighborhoods and be capable of effecting "quality education" for Muslim children – receive the education we are all paying for out of our tax dollars. Why pay again for what we are being taxed for? Every other ethnic group does this.

Aahhhhhhh, we are talking "culture" again. It is no secret that most of our Muslim schools are substandard. Who are we kidding? Ourselves. Only ourselves. You have a system in place – the public school system. Target your area and take it over by the peaceful means described herein.

Necessarily, the chosen area would likely (and practically) be an area in which many Muslims already live. This is upon the people and their leadership. Everyone wants lots of money and no-one wants to work (hard). Everyone wants success but the same people are afraid of failure. Everyone wants to go to Heaven but everyone is afraid to die. So things remain the same! Except Death.

Running a quality school system is hard work and takes big-bucks annually. May All Mighty Allah bless everyone who has ever made a sincere contribution toward Islamic Education. Ameen. This is honestly my prayer for them.

But the truth of the matter is that most people who work hard to develop these schools are not the legitimate Islamic Leaders. Usually the Islamic Leader, if there is one, goes along for the ride because he has not effected control over his people, then their school becomes their community.

This is incorrect. Your 'controlled/governed' neighborhood ushers in *your* controlled school system. There is no intelligent need to 'find a building to convert into a school.' To attempt to develop a school system bereft of a neighborhood is an exercise in futility. The neighborhood must logically come first.

There is another way to look at this. Why should one Muslim even think that his child deserves a special education and his brother's child does not because his brother cannot afford the tuitions? I repeat, this or that schooling is not necessary but we all have to have a roof over our heads. Muslims must develop neighborhoods and target the public schools within their neighborhoods.

Initially, as Muslims move in, non-right living people will move out and the Muslim community will grow. Liquor stores, drug dens, prostitution, crime in general will move out with them. Muslim businessmen are waiting to fill the void; waiting for a community to serve.

At this point I will direct our reader to read *Black Economics* by Dr. Jawanza Kunjufu.[1] Aside from the fact that he appears to be comfortably tied into western styled capitalism and Christianity, he never-the-less paints a very concise picture for the black businessman to better understand the arena in which he must compete. His explanation of other people's high rate for success relative to the low success rate for the African-American in his own community is very enlightening. It all points to "culture". What Dr. Kunjufu seems to have omitted is the fact that African-Americans have no independent "culture", the magnet which draws and the glue which binds.

Before concluding, I wish to note that during the past twenty or so years there were two Orthodox Islamic communities in New Jersey which tried to "culturally" embue their people, with relative degrees of success, considering that they were working in a cultural vacuum. They were Baitul-Quraish under the leadership of a man whom I admired, Shaykh Kamil Wadud (Allah have mercy on him) and the Islamic Community of Masjid Baytul-Khaliq.

Separate and apart, they both attempted and succeeded in the development of "tribal naming systems" within each respective Community/Congregation. There were several "major families" within each organization. When a person "accepted/returned" to Islam, they could choose to become affiliated with the family of the person through whom they came into the organization. We try by doing (and Allah knows best).

This was an honest attempt by early leadership to put into use the displaced "family spirit" which everyone needs. The "family spirit" which in most cases became displaced upon one's `acceptance' of Islam.

In conclusion: The task of the Islamic Leader is difficult but the direction is so clear. He must put his trust only in Allah and summon the courage to do the difficult. After the difficult will come the ease. "...Surely there is ease after hardship, most surely there is ease after hardship. So when you are free (from anxiety) (still) strive hard, and supplicate to your Lord earnestly." Qur'aan 94:5-8

To our Muslim masses I say: Never know defeat. Never — even if Life were to give you a `knock-out' punch and leave you laying 'out cold' in the street. You got to get up from there (as soon as you come to) and still believe that you were never defeated! It was just one of life's hard experiences which made you wiser.... never defeated!

Our struggle is life long. You don't win nor lose until it's over. This attitude will remarkably help our brothers be men in their own right and the idea of choosing, accepting and obeying leadership will no longer be threatening to them. Never know defeat!

In closing this segment, I want to state that our task is not an easy one but it is clear. Islam is the answer and Glorious Allah has given us everything we need to be successful... including the will. What I am presenting is a way.

Just think for a moment: African-Americans would not be in the 'sorry' state they are in if the vast majority of them were Orthodox Muslims. They would be a more respected community, viewed from without and within. They would be admired and revered for their overwhelming individual and collective successes. African-Americans would be an asset to America rather than the present burden. They would be much more of an asset today than they ever were in its past. They would in fact be "Americans" and would have given all Americans a clearer God-conscious-ness. This can be our destiny!

"Surely Allah changes not the condition of a people until they change what is in their hearts......" Qur'aan 13:11

CHAPTER 3
SPORTS, ENTERTAINMENT AND INTELLECTUALISM

ES: Imam Abdallah, As-salaamu 'alaykum.

Imam: Wa-'alaykumus-salaam wa rahmatullah.

ES   Imam, continuing along in our series entitled, "Islamicizing of America" some non-Muslims may take your words to mean that Islam is the best religion and go on the defensive and refrain from hearing our message. What is your concern and response?

Imam: The best way is God's way. God, All Mighty Allah, has already answered this question in the Qur'aan. Therefore it is not about "religions", it is about choosing that which leads to upright conduct of the individual and of society as a whole; about what pleases God.

Relative to Christianity, Judaism, Mazdaism, ect., we are saying that these "religions" have become obsolete and were never complete in themselves. Anyone who contends with us on the basis of Christianity verses Islam, I remind them that Christians and Muslims are (both) awaiting the return of Jesus (peace be upon him) and when he returns all things will be made clear. Therefore let us exercise 'patience' which was defined by my dear brother and teacher, Shaykh Ibrahim Isma`il (may Allah have mercy upon him), as "working while waiting without worrying". So let us get to the work at hand and call our shots as we see them.

Good solid moral values should be acceptable regardless of where they are found. In going after them we will invariably have to look toward Islam because Islam is the foremost system we have 'in place' to combat today's social ills in a realistic manner. Let me also remind you that Islam is not a "religion"! It is a way of life.

Prophet Muhammad (PBHU) is reported to have said that every child is born in the natural state (state of Islam) and later his parents make him Christian, Jew, etc. The God's last prophet was sent to set us on the right course without man-made deviations of "religion". Islam has a "flavor" which people like, and once they have tasted it, they seldom abandon it. It is natural.

The basic form of American Government is sound. What it needs is good solid mainline fundamental Judeo/ Christian/Islamic moral implementation which will bring about a self restructuring. This 'restructuring', in and of itself, will create the means of imposing certain naturalrestraints on the basic freedoms we all enjoy or wish to enjoy. No one to excess, nor at another's expense.

Why "fundamental (mainline) Jewish/ Christian/ Muslim"? Because this is a multi-religious society and Muslims already acknowledge the authenticity of the prophets of the former, and because all three ascribe to "related revelation" (by agreement or disagreement), and as well as the fact that all three represent the dominant "religious" populations of American Society.

America has lofty ideals which are really based upon a Judeo/Christian ethic. That's no secret. These ethics are based upon the commands of God. Which is why, in our opinion, we find some relative degree of success, although America's religious conscience fails so miserably when she should be achieving so much more!

America needs a strong infusion of Islam, though everyone who is, may wish to remain Jew or Christian with their own established "religious" institutions. America's ideals are of righteousness and the triumph of good over bad, ideals of treating one's fellow with equality and fairness. Islam takes those exact same principles and paints a realistic plan for application. Islam can show America the way, nay, it can get America to applying and elevating these Judeo/Christian ethics into an everyday collective reality.

The Muslim's concern is not to eradicate either of the former. God's plan will be what it will be and no one can change that. However, Muslims are prepared to show Americans that in their best form toward attaining their lofty ideals, they are in fact Muslim in their hearts.

"Those who believe (in the Qur'aan),
Those who follow the Jewish (scriptures),
 And the Sabians and the Christians,
Any who believe in Allah (God),
And the Last Day,
And work righteousness,
On them shall be no fear,
Nor shall they grieve."   Qur'aan 5:72

Islam makes a man ever conscious of his mortality. We are reminded that we are born to die; our deeds of the interim we carry around our necks. Just recently I viewed a movie (a comedy). One of the principles portrayed himself as Jesus (peace be upon him) in what appeared to be the famous painting entitled "The Last Supper". This was casually done in a particular scene in which said character was lecturing to a group of his "disciples" while standing in front of said painting. All for a laugh.

Islam would not permit it and Muslims in general would never knowingly stoop to this nor any other type of debasement of their way of life, nor tolerate it! If a person, a people, a nation, does not have anything which it holds sacred, then it is surely doomed.

Our talks on this occasion shall cover sports and

entertainment. We shall state the case, give observations and present solutions. Insha'Allah.

As most of our readers know, our organization places a premium value on leadership and leadership development. African-Americans need be directed by their respective leaders to stop so much dancing and singing, and turn their energies in the direction of intense/focused study of the arts, computer and advanced electronics, aeronautics, medicine, the philosophical, social and techno-logical sciences, etc.

Admittedly, many preachers would be out of busi-ness if not given their 'stage' on which to entertain, but the concern today from the pulpit and mimbar is to preach, teach and lead. To teach people how to have a positive impact upon their own destiny; to teach to them about it and to lead them to it. Only the leaders among the preachers will succeed because a leader will accomplish more than just leading people back and forth to church. He will lead them forward into life.

Let us look at a contemporary scenario: A newly elected President is filling his cabinet. When his actions say there are no African-American candidates, what he honestly is claiming is that there are no African-American candidates, of the few available, who meet his qualifications. And this is his right! Yes.... there are a few African-Americans who are qualified, probably over-qualified. However, there are too, too few of them. Therefore, when a president or corporate executive looks for someone to help him run the country or the corporation, he has got to go for those whom he feels confident in; for whatever reason. In the final analysis it is about making himself "look good". Race, color, creed, religion, etc. is not going to over-ride that factor and, in truth, must have no bearing for the success of the organization! There need be a "pool" of qualified African-

Americans in every intellectual endeavor.

In sports and entertainment, African-Americans like Willie Mays and Jackie Robinson have added excitement to these industries by their natural abilities. This natural excitement is what led to their increase in numbers despite the color of their skin.

We are saying that the world of "intellect" (beyond that which motivates physical abilities), the world of planning, developing and producing, needs to be "excited" by our incursions.

African-Americans need real leaders, but they have been conditioned not to seem overwhelmingly concerned about this. Not concerned enough to effect change. Why? Because they continue to be controlled by their nafs (low desires). In truth, African-Americans can ill afford to be morally weak like most Americans. All Mighty Allah Says: "The life of this world is but sport and play: But if you believe and guard against evil, He (God) will grant you your recompense, and will not ask you (to give up) your possessions." Qur'aan 47:36 (Y. Ali Trans/note) ¹

What is meant here is that: #1 – Amusement and play are not bad things in themselves. As preparations for the more serious life, they have their value. But if we concentrate on them, and neglect the business of life, we can not prosper. So we must use our life in this world as a preparation for our spiritual or inner life. And #2 – Complete self-sacrifice, if voluntarily offered, has a meaning. It means that the person's devotion is exclusively and completely for the cause. But no law or rule can demand it. And a mere offer to kill yourself has no meaning.

You should be ready to take risks to your life in fighting for the cause, but you should aim at life, not death. If you live, you should be ready to place your substance and acquisitions at the disposal of the cause. But it is not reasonable to pauperize yourself and become a hanger-on for the cause. Moreover, the inborn tendency to self-preservation in an average man would lead to concealment and niggardliness if all (everything) were asked for the cause, by law, and there would further be a feeling of bitterness and rebellion.

The entertainment industry and the sports industry have made millionaires out of many African-Americans. So what has it profited the masses? Nothing but to lead them further astray. How many Bill Cosbys or Oprah Winfreys are there? Too, too few. How is all of their money being spent? Mostly by low moral, hell raising, big hat wearing and big car driving self indulgers. How many interest-free, economic banks have been established? How many business training academies have been established for up and coming inner-city entrepreneurs?

Again, how many economic banks have been established? How many free neighborhood clinics have been established and maintained? How many economic banks and credit unions have been established? How many African-American real estate consortiums have been established? Where are the special schools for talented African-Americans?

A national program of selling blood pressure medicines to ourselves (and others) at discount prices through a national prescription plan similar to that of the American Association of Retired Persons would continually fund economic bank projects around the country. Where are our noted physicians, pharmacists and politicians? Where is African-American inter-professional cooperation? Why have not these overwhelmingly Christian African-Americans consolidated their financial strength and collective influence in order to give a token of something back to their trapped brethren. Why has there been virtually no Manly/Womanly stand up for freedom of self from among them? Why not?

Because these people are independents and believe that they alone are responsible for their successes. They have no real leadership in their lives nor backgrounds! They are independents. Some may give a casual thanks to God while simultaneously living a life of sin.

African-Americans can no longer tolerate these "Independents". They have proved to be worthless to what should be the greater cause — racial freedom and justice in America.

The structure of society is in three general classes:

1. The controllers of society (3%). They are the mega-rich representing corporate America and World Bank executives. They are the controllers of systems of government.

2. The super rich. The large wealthy class (12%) that has realized the American dream. This group includes the successful entertainment and sports industry people who are promoted as idols (something which is worshipped) by the top 3% to keep the bottom 85% in check.

3. The overwhelmingly large class (85%) of people who are the laborers, toilers, dreamers and cannon fodder of society. They tend to depend upon newspapers and TV for their relevant information. They read novels and support live theater, go to the movies and sporting events. These people tend to be set in their ways. Their heads are buried in the sands of life. They do not want nor envision change. They are the backbone of society.

This is a predominantly European-American grouping, but not exclusively so. About as many are employed as not, for various reasons. Overwhelmingly, this group lives day to day in order to survive that they may continue to satisfy their passions. God is seldom in mind.

The controllers use sports as the real religion/opiate of the people for their own capitalistic gains. For example: sports are the primary means for keeping young men in a state of readiness for war. Sports are used from grade school level, on into the pros to maintain a jingoistic public attitude. Yet the shooting sports are not publicly promoted! In fact, the media and the professional politicians are in a conspiratorial confederacy against the public on this point. Why? Because whenever a government (the rich and their politicians) fears the populace, and knowing its own evil actions, it seeks public disarmament. This is historical.

Politicians are the servants of major corporations such as banks, each of the American armed forces, American security forces, ITT, AT&T, pro team owners (baseball, football, hockey, basketball, etc.), GM, Ford, Chrysler, the cigarette industry, the liquor industry, aerospace and transportation industries, communications industry, the arms industry, etc. The money which is paid to entertainers, athletes and top corporate executives pales in comparison to the monies they generate for the corporate owners and CEO's.

The controllers shape opinion through their various controlled media: TV and movies (not the actors but the top echelon of these industries), news journals, etc. The masses of people are kept pre-occupied with some entertainment and/or a ballgame for every season while the affairs of their government are going out of control. The controllers continue to throw out these various forms of exploitation and mind-domination as forms of entertainment which consumes the masses who have been conditioned to submit to their low desires.

Even our children have come to believe that they must constantly be entertained. There is an anonymous quote which says: "If you want to hide something from black people, put it in a book!" For example: When a new movie comes out, you will hear people say that they have got to see this movie. Got to see a movie! But if one doesn't see it, what happens? What? Nothing! But one has been bombarded with so much hype about seeing some trash which one could have easily missed and never known of!

This is purposely done by those who program the action, the controllers of society. Those who have the control to shape, mold, maneuver, twist and/or corrupt public opinion, and the national/international outlook, do so for their own advantages and concerns which are most times bereft of any moral considerations and almost always selfish. Running things for them means being in a position in life with the power at their disposal to control and direct the actions of the world's governments.

Successful African-American entertainers and sports personalities should organize around the concept of "Personal Ethnic Upliftment." They must emplement the economic banks and credit unions for self and qualified entrepreneurs. And until such time as they begin to think and act along these lines, the African-American leaders might adopt the following course of immediate action.

PLAN: Initially (and immediately) implement a twenty-year (a generation) moratorium on professional sports and entertainment. By this, we mean that professional sports and lewd entertainment becomes taboo. Boycotted. Any among the group who goes beyond his educational needs to play sports is ostracized by the group.

Naturally this must be a group decision. Proposed and endorsed by its leadership seeking a 95% success rate. Stop laughing – with no pain there is no gain. A struggle without a struggle is no struggle. So why call it one if one is not prepared to? Leadership?

Allah Most High says: "What is the life of this world but amusement and play? But verily the Home in the Hereafter, – that is life indeed, if they but knew." Qur'aan 29:64

Sports/educational scholarships will continue, provided the student is advancing educationally and intellectually. That some come out of professional sports to contribute to society such as Allen Page (former All-Pro with the Minnesota Vikings) who is Justice-Elect to the Minnesota Supreme Court is refreshing and should be applauded. The African-American has proven that he is physically inferior to no one and clearly physically superior to most. Now he must prove to himself first, and to the world, that the same is also true of him intellectually.

Concerning sports, the average male African-American knows the stats on every player in each league. How does this knowledge benefit him? It doesn't. It is imperative that he begin to know, nearly as well, the specs concerning the production methods of various industries.

Let us take the aerospace industry: It seems that the top level of management includes no African-Americans. This absence does not mean that all of this was accomplished without African/African-American help, knowledge and expertise. Having all European faces and minds to the near exclusion of African faces and minds is a power statement of their superiority in this field which the African-American allows to continue by his inaction or (up until now) incorrect action.

The need for redirection of effort is clear. The time is now. Not to act at this time in our history, in a revolutionary way, is to condemn African-American Intellectualism to being meaningless and ineffectual.

Let us touch on the subjects of music and entertainment.

Some of man's most astounding genius is exhibited though the medium of entertainment. Music should be appealing and appeasing to the spirit and the gentle emotional nature of the soul. Music should not appeal to man's baser instincts. The direction of music and entertainment in general must be ethnically monitored so as to close the doors for destructive elements and influences to gain entrance into the fabric of society (of which TV is already integral).

Most things we hear in today's music, if you can understand what is being said, either does not make any sense, or it is so lewd, profane and vile that it should not be listened to by decent people anywhere at anytime. The same with comedy and other forms of entertainment: Lewdness and outright vulgarity is not an art form. It is Satan playing upon our baseness of character with low class thought forms. Laughter can be excited by pleasantness and gentle exercise of the intellect, and even if somewhat risqué at times. Bill Cosby will never be outclassed by those such as Eddie M., or Richard P., Redd F., nor any of the new "cussin' cable comic clowns". Why? Because his material and reputation reflects decency and theirs reflects the opposite. The same for the movies and live theater.

The fact that there is a market for lewdness is an indictment of society. Music has no color boundaries, and music/melody is ancient to all peoples. In pagan societies, man more often than not has exploited his woman through music, nakedness and ceremony. Again, I say, Yes, Yes, Yes; the African-American is in a bad way. His so-called leaders have helped him perpetuate his general failure.We must all realize that there are no easy ways out of this dilemma (which has now become a problem) and what must be emphasized upon the leadership and upon the following is the understanding that you may not be responsible for the condition you find your self in, but you are the principal one responsible for getting yourself (selves) out of it and into something better. You must do it!

Isn't it stupid to believe that the oppressing hand will do it for you? Leadership? First this means control of one's self. Control of one's baser self. Control of one's sexual self. Control of one's sexual self is not control of the heart, but control of lowly desires. Orthodox Islam is the answer.

Let us take a current scenario: the recent U.S. Navy "Tailhook" sex scandal. The men (pilots) should not have been individually indicted. The organization must be indicted. These men are our warriors on standby, ready to protect this country in a magnificent way. The men and their machines (airplanes, computer/radar guidance systems, etc.), the teachers and designers are all very specially talented people who have, knowingly or unknowingly, benefited from the knowledge of many peoples of all races. It is the hypocrisy, the clash of lifestye and feigned cultural values of the dominant society which would put women into the midst of these warriors, all of whom emanate from a morally starved society!

Indict the organization and let society begin to indict itself. This simply means recognition of the problem and bringing the reality up close for every citizen, rather than allow the beauracracy of organization (government) to distance the 'problem' from the individual citizen. Presently, the governing authorities, all of whom also emanate from a morally starved society, rather than face the responsibility of guiding, fathering and leading the citizenry, acquiesce to their baseness of self and perform a circus act of public straffing of individuals who 'got caught'! This is hypocritical political meandering at its worst, which shows why no government can honestly function on behalf of its people and exclude the moral religious aspect of their lives in its every decision.

If, to a God-conscious people its government is not foremost concerned with serving God, how can this government serve them? How can it be concerned with protecting them and not their souls which collectively is the soul of the nation? Allah says: "It was We who created man, and We know what dark suggestions his soul makes to him: for We are nearer to him than his jugular vein." Q 50:16 Allah also says: "...the human soul is certainly prone to evil..." Qur'aan 12:53

Knowing this as we do, we must come to understand that the human soul is like a child who basically knows right from wrong. However, the childlike quality of the soul must be controlled and guided by the parent of intellect so as to keep it from destroying itself. All Mighty Allah says:
"By the Soul, and the proportion and order given to it;
And its enlightenment as to its wrong and its right;
Truly he succeeds who purifies it,
And he fails that corrupts it!"   Qur'aan 91:7-10

The U.S. President and Congress would do well to include on their agenda an official look and study into the past most glorious moral societies; and publicly postulate what aspects may prove useful in our present day society. Right off, the moral consideration will eliminate most. If one does not look to the best to choose from, how does one choose? Does one or does one not learn by past mistakes? Does one not light a candle to dispel the darkness of the times? Or, does one simply continue to stumble in the dark? We have heard of artificial intelligence but what we also have is artificial ignorance. This is a manifestation of man's refusal to use his God-given intelligence which will testify for or against him on Judgement Day (as to how he used it).

41

Let us consider another scenario: A young girl/woman goes out on a date and is raped. Does the public have the right to believe and expect there will be no emotional/ sexual relationship between these two? How can anyone believe that the female and her date are to get involved, perhaps have petting sessions, and there be no sexual loss of control? Instead of being out on a date, she should be home or somewhere behind a veil if she didn't want to be raped!

While that last comment may seem extreme to some, even a middle course will call for a cessation of certain recent immoral freedoms. Prophet Muhammad (peace be upon him) is reported to have said that "when two people of the opposite sex come together who are not married to each other, Satan becomes the third party."

Islam gives practical guidance. American society must cease being a society which invents crimes of immorality to be committed and then seeks to punish those who do. This in itself is immoral and hypocritical. Entertainment and sports encourage open mingling of the sexes. While mingling cannot be altogether done away with for every occasion, there must be a moral basis for all of our actions; especially publicly. There must be a redirection of our public policy from general mingling to general separation of the sexes. This will immediately have an effect on crimes induced by licentiousness.

Foolish people try to make men and women equal. They are not. Neither is equal to the other. They are both special and have special roles. All Mighty God says: "Men are appointed guardians over women, because Allah has made the one of them to excel the other, and because the men spend of their wealth (in support of women). So virtuous women are obedient and safeguard, with Allah's help, matters the knowledge of which is shared by them with their husbands..." Qur'aan 4: 34

Raw music affects our intellect. Although Plato made note of such in his *Republic*, this knowledge predates him. Music is primeval in its relationship to the human being and thusly affects his soul. In truth, we will never be rid of music. However, because of its negative effects upon people, Islam has ordered us to have and maintain control over it, due to its inherent beastly quality and its ability to attract evil forces. Let us not forget that music is a creation of All Mighty Allah. Even songs have powers of their own. Nothing makes it easier to comprehend the inherent and influencing quality or spirit of inanimate things than music.

Let me pose the following to you, of yourself. You are in your house, maybe in your bedroom tidying up. You begin to sing a certain song. Maybe you are singing it over and over again. You leave the room. Maybe you leave the house. You are gone for several hours. When you return home and immediately upon re-entering the bedroom you again begin to sing the same song of hours earlier! Has it ever happened to you that the spirit in a song, a tune, a verse, layed in wait for your return!?

Music makes one more physical in type. For example: In life's varied situations one does not win every encounter. Some are won, some are lost. Everyone understands this reality. Unfortunately, this fact only rings true for many people when they are standing over their vanquished foe, or are looking up at one's victor! Both, bloody, bruised. In reality we have non-physical encounters regularly. It is here where we exercise restraint; we win some, we lose some. The more mad music is absorbed, the more one is being oriented away from rational thought and thought patterns which become acutely affected during intense verbal encounters. Look at the senseless violence among African-Americans. It happens more often than not that among these violent-death-connected people we find more singers and dancers than we find students and scholars. Need I say more? Need anyone say more?

All of you singing and dancing African-American people, look at your communities. Look at your condition. Do you want a change? It will only happen when African-American leadership comes upon a real plan (like previously outlined), that by its pure efficiency will curtail so much singing, dancing and party-game-playing; and direct most all of your resources to the "struggle", thereby turning the tide of our stunted intellectualism.

Therefore, the time has come for African-American religious leaders of every persuasion to reassess the correctness of their individual mission. We Muslims are not saying that the intent of African-American Christian leadership is based upon insincerity. By no means. We believe that most every religious leader is sincere and has abundant faith. What we are saying, however, is that Islam is the only valid way of life for us and the past proves it! It is complete. It represents the completion of God's message, as this humanity knows it, from Adam, through Abraham, Moses, Jesus and Muhammad (PBUT).

We are not saying that any one of these men were "better" than the other. All were pure, wholesome men unguilty of immorality, as God would not choose weak role models for us. We are saying that the role of MuHammad (pbuh) was more extensive than the combined roles of the others and, in that way he had to be, and was, a very special man. A leader among men. The leader of the Prophets by God's command. Personal research on the part of the reader will open one's mind and heart, if Allah so wills.

"Alif, Lam, Rah. These are the ayats (signs) of revelation of a Qur'aan that makes things clear. Again and

44

again will those who disbelieve, wish that they had bowed (to God's Will) in Islam. Leave them alone to enjoy (the good things of this life) and to please themselves: Let (false) hope amuse them: soon will knowledge (undeceive them)." Qur'aan, 15:1-3

Why is God's law so important for us to live by? Because Allah knows that man is most concerned about justice, freedom and equality when it comes to himself. But all men readily acknowledge that one should want for anyone else as one may want for oneself. This is right thinking. This is the thinking of God-consciousness, because it is so easy to be at another's mercy. Therefore, because men do continually evolve in the direction of that which, in fact, they never become (angelic), they are not in a rightful position to judge another except by God's law. Only God's law is indeed concerned with peace, liberty and justice for all. Free of prejudice. So let us put that argument away and deal with problems common to us all. With this straightforward approach it becomes necessary to focus on a source and system of relief from our personal and social agonies: We therefore present the indisputable thesis that Islam has all of the answers by which America may attain her lofty ideals.

Clearly America is not a "melting pot". If America was such, there would be an absolute unmanageable crossing of "color lines". It is much easier, socially and politically, for anyone to cross religious lines by their profession and/or conduct. Allah, The Most High says: "Know you all, that the life of this world is but sport and play, pomp and mutual boasting and multiplying (in rivalry) among yourselves, riches and children. Here is a similitude: How rain and the growth which it brings forth, delight (the hearts of) the tillers; soon it withers; you will see it grow yellow; then it becomes dry and crumbles away. But in the Hereafter is a penalty severe (for the devotees of wrong).

45

And forgiveness from Allah and His Good Pleasure (for the devotee of good). "And what is this life but goods and chattels of deception?" Qur'aan 57:20

Many of the attractive vanities of this world are only traps set by Satan to deceive man. The only real and lasting thing in this life is the decent life lived in the light and spirit of God.

CHAPTER 4
MORAL RELATIONSHIPS – MARRIAGE AND SEX

ES: Imam Abdallah, As-salaamu 'alaykum.

Imam: Wa-'alaykumus-salaam wa raHmatullah.

ES: Imam Abdallah, in this installment of our on-going series entitled "Islamicising America" we know that you plan to focus on "Marriage and Sex".   However, we would like for you to also cover the pre-marital relationship of the Muslim man and the Muslim woman. We have found that too many Muslims are totally in the dark on this aspect of the "marriage relationship" and consequently, their behavior is totally out of sinc with Islamic values.

Imam: Okay. Al-Hamdu lil-laah (The praise be to Allah) that you have brought up this all important aspect of the marital relationship. We must call it an aspect of the marital relationship because of the simple fact that the way in which couples begin their relationship has a tremendous bearing on the quality and continuity of their islamic practice and they will invariably use such practice, rightly or wrongly, during the period of their marriage, to influence other marriageable Muslims with whom they interact.

        First: Men and women who are not married to each other should not engage in free and unrestrained social intercourse with each other. This is clearly a real problem with western society which is a society without restraint. Our beloved Prophet Muhammad (Peace Be Upon Him) has warned all peoples who are concerned with righteousness that when a man and a woman who are not married to each other (excepting the woman's MaHram, a term to be explained in detail further in the text), that when they meet in private, Satan becomes the third party! The results of which none of us are ignorant.

This hadith (tradition of the Prophet, PBUH, which offers guidance for the human-being) places the man, particularly, in a position in which he must exercise restraint against his lower nature so that he does not live a beastly life, acting like an animal which does not know morality. Islamic values teach and guide man (and woman). People who are controlled by their lower nature do not believe that they need to be told or guided and consider such moral guidance an affront to their intelligence. But true intelligence is not mental, it is of the heart; it is correct knowledge of God. For any one who wishes proof of this axiom, I request only that they look at the world today. It is in shambles, yet it is ruled by men of great intellectual (mental) ability, but who have no intelligence of the heart.

The Prophet Muhamad (PBUH) is reported to have said that there is a piece of flesh in the body that if it be pure, then the whole body is pure, and if it be corrupt then the whole body is corrupt. This piece of flesh is the heart.

Man has proven that he is incapable of ruling himself and need accept the rule of a higher authority—God! For man must realize that he is a created thing and needs the guidance of his Creator. Trying to live life without His guidance is like giving a person a computer without the book of instructions and telling him/her to "go at it!" Life would be a series of errors... which is exactly what it is for most people. Most people barter guidance for error in their refusal to acknowledge God as He has prescribed they do. Allah does not accept personalized forms of worship.

When a Muslim, man or woman, desires to meet someone with the hope of meeting a possible marriage partner, there is an Islamic procedure. Basically it goes as follows. The woman informs her wali (lawful guardian) or her wakeel (agent). The man, on the other hand, reaches out for her representative, who would be one or the other.

Many times a Muslim woman will have ignorantly chosen a wali of her choice from among the ignorant Muslim men whom she may have met, here or there. This is totally incorrect. The only person who can be a wali for her is a maHram. A maHram MUST be a Muslim male who is related to her in such a way that marriage between them is absolutely forbidden; such as her father, grandfather, uncle, brother and only under certain circumstances, her adult son. If these people are not available, then it can only be the head of her organized Community/Congregation which is representative of the Islamic State. No one else is lawful, which is why it is of paramount importance that she joins unto such an organized group and resigns from the Community Of The Street. This is where her protection lies.

Unfortunately, far too many Muslims belong to The Community Of The Street and consequently their spiritual leader is Satan. According to the four Orthodox Islamic Schools of Law it is unlawful for a woman to marry without a guardian.[1] However, the Hanifi school gives her a bit more independence, while the Prophetic tradition makes it clear that even in such a case the Ruler is in fact her guardian. And what must be realized in looking at this Hanifi viewpoint, is that the woman, in a land governed by this School of Law, is still surrounded by her Muslim family, and family is going to look after and protect its own from harm.

Not withstanding the foregoing, for those Muslims who do not ascribe to a particular School of Law, it is most intelligent to accept the majority viewpoint as it is highly unlikely that they would have agreed in error. If the Amir (overall organizational leader) is her recognized representative, he may very well choose a wakeel to represent her in his stead because of his limitations in representing so many women. This is usually someone whom she also approves of and it is most proper that he be married and that she has ready and simultaneous access to he and his wife for proper Islamic advice and guidance. This wakeel still does not have carte blanche rights of unlimited association with this female.

Once the Muslim man or woman makes known his or her interest in someone, her agent will be informed and make the necessary arrangements for the two of them to meet. It may take several meetings. They may see one another at gatherings but never in seclusion. This is her protection. The man should be honorable enough not to try to circumvent this program by romancing her in private settings or on the telephone. She, in turn, should be honorable and trusting in her representative because it takes a man to deal with a man, as men and women are not the same, they do not see things the same way.

ES: Imam Abdallah, there are many people, including Muslims, who would disagree with you on this point. Consequently, many Muslim women have adopted the "Feminist" attitude of Western Society.

Imam: These people are ignorant. All of them. Point of fact: Many times one has heard a woman say about another woman that she feels a certain way about such woman because she is a woman and knows how women think. Well, to my dear sisters I can only say that one woman knows another about as well as men know each other. It is reported that the Prophet Muhammad (PBUH) said: "If man knew what thoughts ran through his brother's mind, he would not bury him when he died." That is deep. Something women can't begin to comprehend.

Before leaving the subject of the "MaHram", let me

add the following in order to reiterate its importance: humanity's last Prophet, Muhammad (PBUH) is also reported to have said that the brother-in-law is The Death. In other words, even the brother should not be alone with his brother's wife! In another hadith (prophetic tradition) the father-in-law is also called The Death. The father in-law also should not be alone with his son's wife. Neither the son-in-law nor the father-in-law are proper guardians for a woman. In fact, so severe is the second circumstance that if the father-in-law were to commit adultery with his son's wife, the marriage between the woman and his son is immediately terminated, forever.

Now, in pointing out the fallacy of those ignorant people who would attempt to "unify" the sexes by having women playing the role of men, vis. a vis. policemen/policewomen, firemen/firewomen, soldiers and soldierettes.... please allow me to shed light on the folowing. The primary biological/genetic difference between men and women, besides the obvious, is one of courage. There have been countless untold numbers of men, from all regions of the earth, throughout history, who have faced eminent or certain death, in battle or otherwise, with the most stoic examples of courage. Women cannot do this. Women were not created to perform in this manner. Oh yes, there are always exceptions to the rule, and I'm sure we have all heard of Amazons and Wonder Woman, but when was the last these people visited your neighborhood?

In all seriousness, as a rule this matter of courage is not a female characteristic in the same vein as it is for men. Man is a warrior. Man's history bears witness to this fact. This quality is necessary for does not Allah (SWT = SubHana Wa Ta`ala = The Glorious and The Most High) tell us in Qur'aan that were it not for some men repelling others that even places of His worship would be destroyed (by evil warriors)? Yes!

"For had it not been for Allah's repelling some men by means of others, monasteries and churches and synagogues and mosques, wherein the name of Allah is often remembered, would assuredly have been pulled down. Verily Allah helps one who helps Him. Surely Allah is Strong, Almighty..." Qur'aan 22:40

"Allah has purchased from the believers their lives and their wealth because the Garden (Paradise) will be theirs: They shall fight in the way of Allah and shall slay and be slain. It is a promise which is binding on Him in the Torah and the Gospel and the Qur'aan. Who fulfills his covenant better than Allah? Rejoice then in your bargain that you have made, for that is the supreme triumph." Qur'aan 9:111

It is not in woman's nature to do this. In today's attempt to equate woman with man on this level, oh yes she appears capable while she is on the winning team. But the truth of the matter is that she is incapable of facing certain death and still battle with total non-restraint until she receives a mortal blow. Not so with man. How many times has a man been insulted and induced to fight or to stand up for himself, by telling him that he is acting like a woman? (MAN, Stop acting like a Woman.) They are two different beings. It is not her nature. Let woman start really dying in combat and watch how quickly they start acting feminine. Allah (SWT) says: "Men are the protectors of women because Allah has given the one more strength than the other (or the ability to excell the other)..." With this I rest my case and prove my point, and leave all still ignorant to their ignorance and to their eventual return to their Creator. Ameen.

In continuum, the wali or the wakeel would arrange

for the parties to meet. However, prior to their meeting he would have met with the prospective husband himself and gathered certain bits of informaton such as the essence of the man's faith and his intentions toward the woman; whether or not he is circumcised, or employed, has his own home, wealth, who are his family, does he intend to remain in the vicinity, is he married or ever been married and what is his current status relative to his mariage and/or divorce, does he have a "problem with his hands", etc. If the man is well known, the woman's representative will check into his reputation. In other words, it is the duty of the wali/wakeel to look out for the woman's interest as best he can, and it is the sensible duty of the woman to let him. It is not yet time for her to fall in love because the simple truth of the matter is that she is as likely to love the next (eligible) man just as much as this one!

People have to learn to trust in Allah and let Allah's plan for them manifest itself, rather than try to make something happen which usually happens detrimentally. The woman must seek her agent's consent although he cannot prevent her from marrying the man of her choice. His job is to help her make a wise choice. However, a dutiful son must never marry someone whom his parents are opposed to. The marrying son or daughter is wise to follow the advice of their parents especially. Generally speaking, the parents know their children and having raised them, know what will make their children happy. Their wisdom is invaluable.

The Prophet Muhammad is reported to have said that a woman is married on account of four reasons: Her beauty, her social status (nobility of her family), her wealth and her character. He advised that a man seek a wife possessing nobility of character (which is magnified through her faith as the other qualities are fleeting). It goes without saying that few if any would want to marry the Elephant Man (or woman) but in truth most people do have a physical beauty. As the saying goes: "Allah don't make no junk!" The physical beauty is a natural attraction which Allah has built into His creation as a means of assuring the continuity of the species but this is not representative of the real beauty of the individual. Unfortunately, too many men and women, young and old, do not possess the mature insight to see beyond the surface and go out of their way to seek surface beauty whereas the real beauty is more often than not beyond the depth of the skin.

The principals now enter into a "state of intentions" to marry while maintaining virtually the same posture of association. The ideal attitude is one of seeking marriage with a suitable partner with the desire to please Allah. The over emphasis of western culture on "getting to know one another" leads to fornication while the truth of the matter is that people do not truly get to know each other until they have lived together and living together without the benefit of marriage is against Allah's injunctions and every avenue which leads to sin must be closed off. For this reason, marriage must not be unduly delayed. Therefore a contract is negotiated and or agreed upon between the parties concerned who may include representatives from both sides.

To be included in the contract is the "maHr" (dowry) which is the free gift which the husband gives to the wife at the time of marriage. The value of the maHr depends upon the circumstances of the husband and the position of the wife; there being no limits, it may be a ring of iron or a heap of gold. Once again the woman's agent must do his job to see that the woman receives her due without being unreasonable. The contract must not apply any Islamically unlawful conditions upon either party. The key is fairness.

I will not burder our readers with the details of respective duties of the marriage partners. I will only say this: The key to a successful marriage is kindness. The husband and wife must be kind to each other. Allah (SWT) has told us through our beloved prophet (PBUH) that he who is not kind to His creatures cannot expect to receive kindness on Judgement Day. Therefore, it only stands to reason that one must be kind to one's familiy first and foremost. Actually, Islam demands this. The Prophet Muhammad (PBUH) is reported to have said that the best of men are they who are best to their wives. The key is "Kindness". Treat one another nice.

ES   Imam Abdallah, what is Islam's position on the plurality of wives; particulary in this society?

Imam: First let us explain what it is that Islam does not sanction and what it does. Islam does not allow polygamy. Islam does, however, sanction polygany. Polygamy is the having plurality of wives or husbands at the same time. Polygany, on the other hand, which is properly pronounced 'pa-lij-a-ny' is having plurality of wives at the same time.The purpose here is to show that there is no controversy on the subject of polygany and that Muslims do not cause a controversy where there is none.   Allah (God All-Mighty, The God, The One and Only God, Allah) says: "If you fear that you shall not be able to deal justly with orphans, marry women of your choice, two, three, or four; but if you fear that you shall not be able to deal justly (with them), then only one, or (a captive) that your right hands possess. That will be more suitable, to prevent you from doing injustice." Qur'aan 4:3

The point here is that All Mighty Allah's words are clear. The reference to "orphans" acknowledges the excess of women as it was after the Battle of Uhud that this ayat was promulgated. After Uhud the Muslim Community was left with many orphans and widows. The clause about orphans simply introduces certain rules about marriage and

55

does not make the rules conditional to orphans, as any scholar knows.

Narrated Urwa (R) that he asked `Aisha (R) about the statement of Allah (SWT): "If you fear that you shall not be able to deal justly with the orphan girls,..." Qur'aan 4:3 (as quoted above) and Aisha said, "O my nephew! (This verse has been revealed in connection with) an orphan girl under the guardianship of her guardian who is attracted by her wealth and beauty and intends to marry her with a MaHr less than what other women of her standard deserve. So they (such guardians) have been forbidden to marry them unless they do justice to them and give them their full MaHr, and they are ordered to marry other women instead of them." Bukhari, Book 7, Page 2, No.2.

Also Allah says: "O you who believe! Make not unlawful the good things which Allah has made lawful for you, but commit not excess: For Allah loves not those given to excess." Qur'aan 5:90 This is a warning from Allah (SWT). This warning is not in reference to food alone, but to all physical pleasures. This warning is from Allah to: "O you who believe." Thus whoever tries to make unlawful that which Allah (The Knower, The Wise) has made lawful, that person is a disbeliever or a hypocrite. He or she is guilty of KUFR (disbelief) and does not believe in Allah's words.

All-Mighty Allah has made polygany lawful. Only a dis-believer would say it is unlawful. Neither I, you, the U.S. Government nor the United Nations of the world can make unlawful that which Allah (SWT) has made lawful. There is only one primary law and it is Allah's Law. All manmade laws must take a back seat to His law and if anyone says that Allah says in The Qur'aan that you must follow or obey the law-of-the-land in deference to Allah's law, ask the liar to show it to you. He can't, and he won't, because Allah would never give an order which even possibly leads to disbelief. For the law of this land approves of and orders many un-Islamic things.

Point of fact: Marriage according to the law of this land is not Islamic. We must all come to understand that a woman in a polyganous situation is simply married. That is all, and panel discussions dealing with her personal situation are wrong. Needless to say, there are good marriages and there are bad marriages. In fact, there are more than enough monogamous marries which need to be tightened up than to enter into useless discussions about polygany!

Necessarily, a successful polyganous situation must encompass the right people. It is not for everyone. Allah has made polygany lawful for the Muslim and has given him the option of doing it or not. Therefore, all our matters are to be decided according to Islamic law, first. The acceptable sources of Islamic law on this subject are:

1 The Qur'aan;
2 The Sunnah (traditions) of the Prophet
   Muhammad (PBUH);
3 Ijma`a;
4 Qiyas;
5 (A) Istisan/ (B) Istislah/ (C) Istishab;
6 Urf....Explanations

Firstly we go to The Qur'aan (The Word of Allah). If we do not find an answer we then look to The Sunnah (Practices of The Prophet and or what he allowed of his Companions). If we do not find the answer there, next we look to Ijma`a, The consensus of the Companions of The Messenger of Allah, Their Successors, The Successors of The Successors and/or the consensus of the Learned Jurists of any day or age.

NOTE: Prophet Muhammad is reported to have said that the first three generations of Muslims would be the best Muslims. They are/were:

1-The Companions of the Prophet

2- The Companion's Successors, and

3- The Successors of the Successors.

It is important to know that during the times of these Muslims, who were the best Muslims, polygany was more of a rule of Muslim life. This shows how far Muslims have deviated from the true path when a regular practice of the best Muslims and of Rasulullah himself is now a cause of debate among today's Muslims who are lesser strivers.

Let us continue. If we do not find our answer through Ijma`a, next we must go to the source of Islamic Law called "Qiyas", which means deduction by analogy. We look back through the first three sources of Law, in respective order, for a similar situation, and if found, we make an analytical analysis by comparing that similar situation to our present situation and based upon the similarities between the two, we can arrive at a decision.

Next, if we cannot use Qiyas, Imam Hanifa said we may use "Istisan" (Preference). Imam Maalik said "Istislah" (Masalihah - Public policy - as he accepted the opinion of the citizens of Madina as a source of Law.) Imam Sha`ifi said "Istishab" (Concordance = Agreement), as he was a bridge between Imam Hanifa (considered the most liberal of the four Sunni/Orthodox Schools of Thought) and Imam Maalik. May Allah be pleased with all of them.

If this does not suffice, we may then use `Urf (Common Law). Anyone who deliberately uses a source of Law out of place or who omits a superior source of law for a lesser source can only be charged with attempting to satisfy his own "nafs" (low desires) and at not attempting to strive toward righteousness. However, on the subject of polygany,

The Qur'aan, our first source of law makes clear Allah's position. What is more is that The Sunnah, etc. supports The Qu'aan.

However, Muslim men should not threaten their present Muslim wives with polygany as a means of "straightening her out". Clearly she has the option of seeking/gaining a divorce! Also, it must be understood that if a Muslim has the basic financial, physical and emotional means, no one can tell him that he cannot practice polygany. Who knows Allah's creation better than Allah. Men are polyganous by nature and All Mighty Allah has provided a means by which he may live a virtuous life while satisfying this nature.

A society which only endorses monogamy is going to be filled with licentiousness, lies, deciet and unbridled deviant sexual attitudes. Look at western society. Only a society based upon exacting maximum profits benefits from promoting monogamy because therein exists the primary concern for money, not concern for people and society. A society based upon Interest, Insurance and Fraud will always promote monogamy.

It should be noted that after the World Wars there were European countries which tacitly endorsed and practiced polygany, and this was tacitly accepted by other western governments until these societies once again became competively stable. Also, considering the rate at which African-American men are killing themselves, being incarcerated and/or accepting deviant life styles, polygany is the only course for the future. There is so much to be said.

ES: Imam Abdallah, the last subject for our current issue is surely to be somewhat controversial. Sex. We are hoping that our readers will put the best construction on what you have to say concerning this.

Imam: I am sure that our readers are mature minded people who recognize that sex is a very important aspect in the total life plan of the human being. However, what is presented is as important as how it is presented.

Firstly, we must ask our readers to ask themselves which are the primary internal reasons why marriages fail. In answering honestly, they will probably name at the top of their list the following: money (financial); compatibility (attitude and sex); associations (family and friends). When asked what are the resources which stabilize marriages they will invariably name the same! And of course, there is always "love". What also must be admitted is that "love" becomes mighty strained when the former three are limited or detrimentally applied.

In short, sex is of primary importance in the lives of married persons, and rightly so. Recognizing this, it seems that it is important for the parties to have some knowledge of sex. Not the sexual experience, but of sexual directions. In my experience of consulting with many men and women, youthful and mature types, over the past twenty plus years, I have seen that lack of sexual gratification is often a cause for unhappiness in marriages and a cause for divorce. This is especially true among young people. We must ask ourselves, "Are there any remedies?"

I also request of the reader to read page 83 of As-Shaykh Maulana Abul A`ala Maudoodi's book entitled *The Laws Of Marriage And Divorce In Islam* in which he reminds us that "Islamic Law has not been designed for heavenly beings but for the common-run of humanity." (May Allah have mercy upon him and bless him.) Again, are there any remedies? I say "yes", and wish to propose the following based upon my observations which have been and are in keeping with Islamic etiquette.

I sincerely believe it is the duty of parents not to

send their children sexually ignorant into marriage.

I propose that parents acquire knowledge of sexual responsibility as it pertains to lawfully satisfying each other sexually and pass this knowledge on, at the appropriate time, to their children; father to son, mother to daughter. The all important matter of correct sexual attitudes is going to be one of America's foremost tests as to its survival or demise.

Today we see the ruination of our children because of loose morals perpetuated within society in the name of "freedom of expression" or "art". Corrupt people (devils) are spreading this corruption; and it starts at the top. By this I do not mean the ruling politicians, who are only highly paid government servants. I mean by their rulers, the controllers of society. American children are not taught abstinence, instead they are now given sexual education and condoms. The health of their minds are forfeit for a feigned concern for health of their bodies; there is an underlying profit motive. It cannot be over emphasized that abstinence is just as important for boys as it is for girls.

The word of God, The Creator, is corrupted in preference to the word of man, the created. This is evil. Certainly, loose sexual morals beget loose and corrupted personal characters. Just listen to the average American school children; their mouths are as filthy as their minds. Needless to say, African-Americans are by far the worse. Parents must seize control of what is taught in the schools; but then again, they too are corrupted because they are the primary villains with respect to God's commandments, and oftimes at home they are their children's worst teachers! Is there any hope? I say, "Yes" realizing that it is always darkest just before the dawn; but, the dawn always comes on time, and it is approaching fast.

So, what must parents do? I suggest that the evil of inter-sexual boy/girl contact be neutralized by the Islamic Code described at the beginning of this article. How can the rank-and-file school children be expected to learn in schools which are no more than dens of physical and deviant philosophical sexual exposure"? Further, if one would not have a foul-mouthed fool over for family supper nor a whore sitting in one's living room for family visitations, why bring them into one's homes over the TV? How is it different?

Parents must teach their children moral values by example. Sure, some filth will slip through the cracks; but a crack is not the same as an open door. America needs Islam and she must be made aware that Islam is not the arch villian of humanity that its enemies are depicting it to be. With the demise of the Evil Empire, which was destroyed not by the west but by Islam through Afghanistan, these enemies are attempting, with relative success, to cast Islam into the void left behind. In truth, Islam is America's silent salvation and its adherents are truly her citizens ever as much so as any people conscious of The One God could ever be.

In conclusion, I further propose in regard to finding a mate for marriage, that Muslims as well as all others, learn to trust in "Qadr" (Divine Destiny) rather than trying to make something happen with someone. This takes patience, something a society without restraints abhors; and patience is akin to abstinence.

CHAPTER 5
CRIME AND PUNISHMENT

ES: Imam Abdallah, As-salaamu 'alaykum.

Imam: Wa-'alaykumus-salaam wa rahmatullah.

ES: Imam Abdallah, in this, our fifth installment under the current heading, "Islamicizing America", we believe the subject of crime, punishment and law enforcement to be of particular concern to all Americans. Will you please begin your discourse allowing the ES to freely interject at specific points.

Imam: This is certainly an area where Americans can utilize a strong Islamic influence. However, the libertinisn of many Americans fosters a hypocrisy which borders on spiritual ignorance. Crime is crime no matter who commits it, for whatever excuse. There can be no reason, only an excuse, and an excuse is nothing but a lie; any excuse. The only valid reason for the commission of an act deemed unlawful by society, is an act to throw off oppression imposed or sanctioned by that society; such oppression being a contravention of the laws of God. All Mighty Allah says in Qur'aan "........Persecution and suppression of opinion by violence is worse than killing." Qur'aan 2:191 (See *The Meaning Of Qur'aan* by Shaykh Abul A`la Maududi, Allah's Mercy be upon him)

        Unfortunately, the so-called Muslim governments of the world are as corrupt as their Western counterparts. Their loss of temporal power and worldly influence through their abandonment of basic Islamic principles along with their attempts to follow the west, has resulted with their rulers, a large percentage of their populations, and their police/security forces becoming just as corrupt as any anywhere. Therefore, these Muslim lands also are in need of an Islamic infusion. The whole world needs it.

Now someone, particularly a non-Muslim American, might ask: "How would Islam vis-a-vis Islamic Law, benefit our society?"

I might begin to answer this question by saying (and then attempting to explain) the following.

1- There would be, in short time, far, far less criminals and resultant crime across the board.

2- There would be, in short time, a move by society to eliminate jails and prisons rather than its constant expenditures to build more.

3- There would be less a need for police/security personnel with a resultant scaling down of forces. This is critical because when we count criminal minds in our society, we must necessarily count those of a large percentage of the land's police/security personnel.

4- The criminal justice system would become unclogged and be in a position to perform its intended purpose; serve Justice.

5- Justice would be fair for all. Thereby, justice would be served.

What follows is not meant to be an indepth expose on Islamic Law, but rather an attempt to show the benefits of an infusion of various aspects of Islamic Law into the American circumstance. For the benefit of many of our Muslim and non-Muslim readers, we list the following prescribed punishments for eight major crimes which are to be implemented in an Islamic State. They are:

1- Rebellion against the Khalifah	=	crucifixion, execution, or exile.
2- Apostacy from Islam	=	execution by beheading
3- Adultery	=	one hundred lashes with a whip and then he or she is stoned to death.
4- Fornication	=	one hundred lashes with a whip, then exile for one year.
5- Drinking alcohol/ intoxication	=	eighty lashes with a whip
6- Theft/denial of a borrowed item	=	Amputation of the right hand
7- Slander by accusing someone of adultry.	=	eighty lashes with a whip
8- Murder	=	Conditionally explained below

The first two conditions clearly would be sanctioned by the Islamic State within its parameters. The latter six are appropriate anywhere. Also, for the student and would-be-student of Islam, the following is given for reference.

ISLAMIC SCHOOLS AND SECTS

1. Orthodox (Sunni) Hanafii
2. Orthodox (Sunni) Maalikii
3. Orthodox (Sunni) Shaafi`ii
4. Orthodox (Sunni) Hanbalii
5. The Extinguished Schools (Zaahirii; Awzaa`ii; Thawrii; Tabarii)
6. Khwaarij or Seceders
7. Mu`tazilah or Dissenters
8. Shii`ah or Partisans

[See "Islamic Jurisprudence In The Modern World" by A. A. Qadry, Pgs.90-173]

Primary Statement: No one in America will, or can, deny that murder, theft, intoxication, adultery and fornication are the foremost crimes and/or causes of social blight in this country and the world. Therefore, my focus will necessarily be in those particular directions.

However, when we look at the subject of punishment, we find an attitude of weakness permeating society. There are perverse groups exporting and propagating ideas foreign to an orderly society, yet they feign wanting to preserve order. They promote the idea that corporal punishment is wrong. They say that this type of punishment is wrong in the home, wrong in the school, wrong through the institutions responsible for administering Justice. They condemn the prudent corporal disciplining of children and the criminal. Then they wonder why so many of their children are becoming criminals, even before leaving the parental home!

For any people who say they believe in God, the law of their land must reflect the wisdom of God. Therefore let us see what God says about punishment. Also, let us suggest that our readers look into the various means of punishment utilized upon the criminals by the prophets of God. Let us not deny that we, as created beings, are so inferior to God, Al-Khaliq (The Creator), that by comparison we absolutely pale into insignificance. Only people of arrogance equate the wisdom of God with their own.

God, All Mighty Allah, tells us in The Qur'aan: "The punishment of those who wage war against God and His Apostle, and strive with might and main for mischief through the land is: Execution, or crucifixion, or the cutting off of hands and feet from opposite sides, or exile from the land: That is their disgrace in this world, and a heavy punishment is theirs in the Hereafter; Except for those who repent before they fall into your power: In that case, know that God

66

is Oft-forgiving, Most Merciful." Qur'aan 5:36 & 37

According to Qur'aanic scholar Shaykh Abdullah Yusuf Ali, for the double crime of treason against the State, combined with treason against God, as shown by overt crimes, four alternative punishments are mentioned in the above verses, any one of which is to be applied according to the circumstances, viz., execution (cutting off the head), crucifixion, maiming (right hand & left foot), or exile. These were features of the criminal law then and for centuries afterwards, except that tortures such as "hanging, drawing and quartering" in English law, and piercing the eyes and leaving the unfortunate victim exposed to a tropical sun, which was practised in Arabia, and all such tortures were abolished.

In any case sincere repentance before it was too late was recognized as a ground for mercy. See Yusuf Ali rendering of Qur'aan, notes 738 & 739. "As to the thief: male and female, cut off his or her hands: A punishment by way of example, from God, for their crime: And Allah is Exalted in Power. But if the thief repent after his crime and amend his conduct, Allah turns to him in forgiveness; for God is Oft-forgiving, Most Merciful. Do you not know that to God (alone) belongs the dominion of the heavens and the earth? He punishes whom He pleases, and He forgives whom He pleases: And Allah Has power over all things." Qur'aan 5:41 & 42

Let us now relate the story of one Fatima bint al-Aswad bin Abdullah who lived during the lifetime of The Messenger of Allah. She was from a very important tribe and a very wealthy and powerful family and clan. Aiysha (Wife of the Prophet....May Allah be pleased with her) reported that the Quraish had been anxious about the Makhzuumii woman who had committed theft, and said: Who will speak to Allah's Messenger about her? They said:

Who dare it, but Usaama, the loved one of Allah's Messenger (PBUH)? So Usaama spoke to him. Thereupon Allah's Messenger (PBUH) said: Do you intercede regarding one of the punishments prescribed by Allah? He then stood up and addressed (the people) saying: O people, those who have gone before you were destroyed because if any one of high rank committed theft among them, they spared him; and if anyone of low rank committed theft, they inflicted the prescribed punishment upon him. By Allah, if Fatima, daughter of Muhammad, were to steal, I would have her hand cut off." This woman had been a habitual thief. However, there was a marvelous change in her after this incident. She calmly submitted to the punishment and though she lost her hand she regained the purity of her soul through sincere repentance and was brought in communion with the next verse (Qur'aan 5:42...."But if the thief repent after his crime and amend his conduct, Allah turns to him in forgiveness; for Allah is Oft-forgiving, Most Merciful.")

The idea behind the punishment is to redirect the soul, with a violent unforgetable shock, back towards God. This is what crime, punishment, and law enforcement is all about. Sh. Abdullah Yusuf `Ali in his Qur'aanic notes 742 & 743 says: In the above verse (41)......" we touch upon jurisprudence. The Cannon Law jurists are not unanimous as to the value of the property stolen, which would involve the penalty of cutting off the hand (right hand for first offense). The majority (Schools of Law) hold that petty thefts are exempt from this punishment. The general opinion is that only one hand should be cut off for the first theft, on the principle that: "Wherefore, if thy hand or thy foot offend thee, cut them off, and cast them from thee; it is better for thee to enter into life halt or maimed, rather than having two hands or two feet to be cast into everlasting fire."

(Matthew 18:8).[1] Apparently in the age of Jesus (Peace be upon him), thieves were crucified (Matthew 27:38). He continues by commenting on the next verse by saying: "Punishment really does not belong to mortals, but to God alone." Only, in order to keep civil society together, and protect innocent people from crime, certain principles are laid down on which people can build up their criminal law.

But we must always remember that God not only punishes but forgives, and forgiveness is the attribute which is more prominently placed before us. It is not our wisdom that can really define the bounds of forgiveness or punishment, but His will or plan, which is the true standard of righteousness and justice." However, it should be clear to all people who claim belief in revelation and The Hour Of Judgement, that evil people must be controlled by society, or they will control society. Certainly, this is their aim. Good being versed by evil is the primary opposing force behind all of man's problems. Allah (The Glorious and The Most High) also says: "Nay, they deny the Hour (Of the Judgment to come): But We have prepared a Blazing Fire for such as deny the Hour: When it sees them from a place far off, they will hear its fury and its raging sigh. And when they are cast bound together, into a constricted place therein, they will plead for destruction there and then!" "This day plead not for a single destruction: Plead for destruction oft-repeated! Say: 'Is that best, or The Eternal Garden, promised to the righteous? For them, that is a reward as well as a goal (of attainment)." Qur'aan 25:11-15

Of these verses Sh. Abdullah Yusuf `Ali says: "Denying the Hour of Judgement means denying the power of Justice and Truth to triumph; it means asserting the dominion of Evil. But the Reality itself will punish them." He continues by describing: "Here the Fire is personified. It is raging with hunger and fury, and as soon as it (The

Hellfire) sees them (the sinners) from a distance ever so far, it emits a *sigh of desire*. Til then they had not realized their full danger. Now, just as their heart begins to tremble with terror, they are bound together – like with like – and cast into the roaring flames!" Therefore we read in Divine Scriptures of Revelation that God is the Most Merciful of those who have the capacity to show mercy. Yet, we are warned that there will be parties of people who will receive the Ultimate Punishment – The Hellfire – based upon how they lived their lives on earth. What is more, some will receive punishment in this life AND the next. Therefore, it can easily be deduced that God All Mighty has put His stamp of approval on appropriate corporal punishment in this life and in the Hereafter.

ES: Imam Abdallah, in your allusion to crime and punishment, you made mention of children in the same sentence along with criminals. Please make a clearer connection.

Imam: Far too many American children grow up in so-called religious homes but are not taught, and made, to pray. Children are the cause of many sins to many parents for a variety of reasons. To prevent this, parents must acknowledge that their duty is to God before it is to their children.

The Prophet Muhammad (PBUH) is reported to have said: "Command your children to pray when they become seven years old, and beat them for it (prayer) when they become ten years old." He is also reported to have said: "When a boy distinguishes right hand from the left, then command him to pray." Besides respect for The Law, prayer teaches man to remember God and to stay in constant communion with Him without an intercessor. Prayer teaches that God is equally approachable and accessible by and to all men. Prayer teaches the unity of humanity. Prayer teaches inward and outward purification of self. Prayer teaches total and complete democracy in its practice. Prayer teaches Muslims to function as one body and to follow one leader. Prayer teaches responsibility, punctuality and discipline in all of our daily activities. Prayer teaches honor and respect for superiors and seniors (their qualities). Prayer teaches intellectual focus and concentration. The benefits of prayer are endless.

Generally speaking, today's children and far too many adults have not been fostered into developing a "God-consciousness". The "Self-Accusing/Self-Reproaching Spirit" is not developed within them and they have little power to check their own evil thoughts before their evil thoughts become evil actions.

Islamic scholars understand there to be three stages of development of the human soul. The first being "Ammaarah" (see Qur'aan 12:53). At this stage the human soul is prone to evil, and if it is not checked, will spread evil around and about and will ultimately destroy itself.

The second stage is called "Al-Lawwaamah" (see Qur'aan 75:2). At this stage of development the soul feels conscious of evil, and resists. It practices repentance and seeks God's forgiveness and tries earnestly to correct and amend its inward and outwardly expressed behavior. The soul is seeking God's pleasure and salvation.

The third stage is "Al-MuTma'innah" (see Qur'aan 89:27), which is the highest stage, and at which the soul has reached a state of righteousness, satisfaction and fulfillment, and is at total peace with its Creator.

The second stage may be compared to "Conscience". However, in the English language "Conscience" is a faculty and not a stage of spiritual growth and development. Most people are hovering somewhere around the second stage. The criminal, more specifically, the career criminal, is immersed in the first stage and if he won't or can't check himself, it is up to the good people of society to keep him/her in check or be victimized by his evil.. The criminal is kept in check by the threat of punishment which must be at least equal to his crime; and the implementation of such punishment, as an exemplary checking device.

ES: Imam Abdallah, many people are opposed to the death penalty for a variety of reasons. Please comment and expound on how this matter might be approached.

Imam: Usually, the death penalty is reserved for the murderer. For those who argue against capital punishment, they should be intelligent enough to understand that the death sentence is protection for each law-abiding citizen. For a potential murderer to know, with certainty, that if and when he is apprehended, his life will be forfeit for the one he has unlawfully taken, will give him second and third thoughts about the commission of said crime. This is society's protection. The rash of murders we witness each day across the nation is indicative that life has little or no value to the murderer because society does not equate his crime with the value of his own life.

What is more, his family should have to pay blood money to the family of the victim. Yes, all immediate family members (grandparents, parents, brothers, sisters, uncles and aunts) will have to collectively pay this debt on behalf of the executed murderer. Pay by lump sum or on installment! When the responsibility is spread across the family spectrum, the impact of acceptable criminal behavior by family members is appreciably diminished.

Murder (qatl) or homicide is classified into five kinds:

1- wilfull murder (qatl-`amd);

2- manslaughter (shubah-`amd);

3- homicide by misadventure (qatl-khaTaa');

4- homicide of the same nature as that of misadventure - (qatl-qaa'im-maqaam-bi-khaTaa'); and

5- homicide by intermediate cause (qatl-ba-sabab).

See Hidaayah, IV, 271 ff.

According to Hanbalii and Shaafi'ii schools, homicide is usually of three kinds: 1- intentional/premeditated; 2- quasi-intentional/voluntary, and; 3- mistaken/involuntary. However, Imam Maalik repudiates the quasi-intentional and puts it into the class of intentional homicide. Manslaughter murders demand compensation/expiation as well as loss of rights of inheritance. In mistaken murders, compensation/expiation and non-inheritance are ordinarily inflicted as punishment and in murders for cause, only compensation is due. Only premeditated homicide involves a penalty under the law of talion (life for life, hand for hand, eye for eye, etc.).

ES: Imam Abdallah, more specifically, being in North America, what about the subject of murder concerning people of different religions?

Imam: The Qur'aan lays down the general principle as an absolute prohibition against murder of any human being: "And kill not the human soul which God has made sacred except in the course of justice" Qur'aan 6:152

It is prescribed that the punishment of retaliation is imposed on every murderer irrespective of religion. The Prophet (Peace be upon him) said: "It is my proper trust (to impose retaliation) in favor of and in faithfulness to the Dhimmees (non-Muslims)" and, with these words he ordered the execution of a Muslim who had murdered a Dhimmee. Abu Haneefah explained the prescriptions provided by the

Traditions of the Prophet (PBUH) and held that Muslims and non-Muslims are held on equal footing before the law of retaliation on the basis of equality accorded to the Dhimmee-contractees in all legal spheres other than personal status, intoxicants and pork." (See *Islamic Jurisprudence In The Modern World*, Anwar AHmad Qadri, Page 294)

ES: Imam, in the aforementioned listing of crimes and Islamic punishments, give an example of like application to the crime of operating a motor vehicle while intoxicated.

Imam: First, let us remind our readers that all punishments must be public for maximum deterrent effect; whether it be execution, cutting off of the thief's hand, or the convicted criminal receiving a certain number of lashes, etc. With great concern today on punishing drunken drivers, let us include an Islamic outlook on punishments for drunkenness (including drug intoxication). After being apprehended and proven intoxicated, he will be publicly whipped for his crime of drunkenness. Also, he and/or his family (as pointed out above) will be responsible for settling any and all debts for loss of life and/or property occurring by him during his state of intoxication.

If he is convicted of drunkedness continually, he may be imprisoned for a specific period of time; not to rule out a life sentence. And/or depending upon the severity of his crimes and disregard for life and law, he may be put to death as he proves himself a murderous menace to society and a financial burden to his family. Society must eliminate him for its own safety as he, in the face of reason, voluntarily puts himself into a murderous and automotive (drunken) state. I make this comment because there is a minority opinion that the drunk person is not responsible for his actions while intoxicated as he is on the level of the animals of the field. Though this is a minority opinion, I take it into

74

cosideration for a society which has legalized an abomination. The drunk driver may get away with his life for one murderous occurrence but not several.

Let us presume that he has lost his license to drive, yet continues to drink and be a murderous menace upon the roadways; how many choices does society have. Also, let us keep in mind that in Islam there is the right of retaliation, whereas the murderer or the attacker is justly subject to have the same injury inflicted upon his person by his victim or his victim's heir. No judge nor jury can mitigate this right and the society which bows to the legalization of alcohol must necessarily bow to it.

Also, for all who are sentenced to prison, it is to be a prison and not a guest house with conveniences. The criminal loses his rights to the luxuries and conveniences of society. If a punishment does not hurt, it is no punishment; and punishment can only be prescribed and meted out by the Judge/Court based upon the Law. Police and security forces are to be punished severely for their arbitrary infliction or application of their own brand of justice. Official abuse of power/authority must never be tolerated. Not to denigrate the many brave, committed and honest police/security personnel, far too, too many police officers/prison guards think exactly like the criminal does, and is often just as costly to society. Far too many of them are more concerned with the public fearing/respecting their fraternity than the law of the land.

This brings up another question: Should the public guardians of the law belong to secret fraternal organizations? I say that they should be exceptionally well educated, trained and well paid parishioners of their respective faiths. Period. Perhaps Americans will once again outlaw alcohol. And perhaps through our proposed Islamic infusion, America will have the moral strength of character to stand by a conviction based upon righteousness. It is absolute folly to legalize alcohol, the worst and most damaging drug of all, and then think that the same people who openly and freely use and abuse one drug (alcohol) are going to rid the country of any others. No intelligent person can realistically think so.

ES: Imam Abdallah, it would not be prudent, to say the least, if we did not address the problem of loose morals in today's society. Fornication and adultery of every kind is rampant. The question is not what Islamic Law has the power to do, but rather, whether the American people have the will to let it do what it can for them.

Imam: Yes. For this society to survive it is going to have to reverse its downward spiral into the abyss of moral decay and debauchery. Open adultery and fornication MUST be eliminated from society. Respect for marriage must be inculcated into the youth at home and in school. Premarital virginity must be respected and honored; for both sexes. Society must stop working overtime to awaken the youthful flames of passion before our youth are ready and into the marriage bond. Society must end the popularizing of sexual exploitation through its various media. I repeat: For this society to survive it must reverse its downward spiral into the abyss of moral decay and debauchery.

Allah, The All Wise, says in Qur'aan: "Come not near to adultery. For it is an abomination and an evil way, opening the road (to other evils)." Qur'aan 17:32

"The whore and the whoremonger, flog each of them with a hundred stripes; and let not compassion keep you from carrying out the sentence of God, if you believe in God and the Last Day; and let some of the faithful witness their punishment." Qur'aan 24:2

Zinaa (fornication and adultery) is among the worst of the world's most heinous crimes. It is committed with either an unmarried or a married person. The punishment for the former (fornication) is not as severe as for the latter (adultery), which calls for the additional punishment of stoning to death (lapidation). Some jurists do not accept it because it is not found in The Qur'aan. However, on the authority of The Traditions, death by stoning is the legal punishment.

Umar, the second successor to the Prophet (May Allah be pleased with him) said: "Verily God sent Muhammad (PBUH) with the Truth and He revealed to him the Book, and amongst that which was revealed to him was the verse on stoning, so I read it, I understood it, and memorized it; and the Mesenger of Allah stoned, and we stoned after him. Therefore, I fear that after a lapse of time, one may say: We do not find stoning in the Book of God, and they would stray by abandoning an obligation imposed by God." Also: On the authority of `Ali, the third successor to the Prophet (may Allah be pleased with him), it is reported that "he lashed Surakhah on Thursday and stoned her on Friday, and he said: `I flogged her in accordance with the Book of Allah and I stoned her in accordance with the Sunnah of the Prophet of God'."

There are many Traditions authorizing stoning. Sh. Abdullah Yusuf Ali says in his Qur'aanic Commentary: "Adultery is not only shameful in itself and inconsistent with any self-respect or respect for others, but it opens the road to many evils. It destroys the basis of the family; it works against the interests of children born or to be born; it may cause murders and feuds and loss of reputation and property, and also loosen permanently the bonds of society. Not only should it be avoided, but any approach or temptation to it should be avoided." Application of this one Islamic Law would dramatically clean up society and direct society to self-eliminate many of the social ills which it has brought upon itself through a reckless drive to create a society without restraint, which is what we have today. Adultery is the foundation of sin and ranks second only to outright rejection of God Himself. Islam not only forbids the sin, but closes off all avenues of approach to it.

God's Laws are for man's guidance. Guidance for His worship and for living our life's experiences with order and peace. Man, around the world, is living in violation to the Law of his Creator. Therefore, is it any wonder that he is out of synch with Nature? As man now looks to reach beyond the the limits of the Earth in his quest for supremacy, how far does he believe that he can go with his reckless abandon and disregard for God's creation, including himself?

Allah tells us in His Book, Al-Qur'aan, that *everything* submits to Him, praises Him, (literally, gives Him His due) except man. Man is indeed an ingrate. We should understand that everything in creation loves God as man should. Is it no wonder that we are witnessing all types of Natural Catastrophe and Biological Epidemics? This is the World Environment fighting back and not submitting to man. Man cannot win this battle. At best he must get the World Environment to back off; and it won't until man learns to control his behavior. It is only the Guidance of God which can help him because he proves every day that he cannot help or control himself by his own means.

CHAPTER 6
BANKING, INTEREST, INSURANCE AND THE ECONOMY

ES: Imam Abdallah, As-salaamu 'alaykum.

Imam: Wa-'alaykumus-salaam wa rahmatullah.

ES: Imam, in this, our sixth installment in our current series, we intend to present to our readers the subjects: "banking", interest, insurance and the economy.   Please begin and the ES shall continue to enjoy the right of interjection when and where it sees fit.

Imam: Yes. However, once again I want to remind our American readers that as unsettling and radical as the inclusion of these Islamic aspects into our western (world) experience may seem, the outcome is geared to promote world peace, security and prosperity, thus allowing the U. S. of A. to live up to her lofty ideals.   This should be the goal of every true American.

ES: Imam, as you well know, many U.S. citizens do not consider themselves Americans by virtue of their "second class citizenship".

Imam: True. However, by virtue of their "accident of birth on these shores", they are American if only in theory. What we have been proposing in this series are ways and means to turn the theory into a practical reality, for everyone. This is what must be striven for if this nation is to long endure. Now, let us get into the subject at hand.

Banking, interest and insurance are so closely related in the present circumstance that they, more often than not, determine the state of the economy. Interest, pure and simple, is unlawful and is a major cause of the world's moral and economic problems.

Allah, The Glorious and The Most High says: "O you who believe! Devour not usury (interest), doubled and multiplied; but fear Alah; that you may really prosper." Qur'aan 3:130

Also: "Those who devour usury (interest) will not stand except as stands one whom The Evil One has driven to madness. That is because they say: Trade is like usury, but God has permitted trade and forbidden usury. Those who after receiving direction from their Lord, desist, shall be pardoned for their past; their case is for God to (judge); but those who repeat (the offense) are Companions of The Fire; they will abide there-in (for ever). Allah will deprive usury of all blessing, but will give increase for deeds of charity: For He loves not creatures ungrateful and wicked. Those who believe and do deeds of righteousness and establish regular prayers and regular charity will have their reward from their Lord: On them shall be no fear, nor shall they grieve. O you who believe! Fear God and give up what remains of your demand for usury, if you are indeed believers. If you do it not, Take notice of war from God and His Apostle: But if you turn back, you shall have your capital sums: Deal not unjustly and you shall not be dealt with unjustly. If the debtor is in difficulty, grant him time until it is easy for him to repay. But if you remit it by way of charity, that is best for you if you only knew. And fear The Day when you shall be brought back to Allah. Then every soul shall be paid what it earned, and none shall be dealt with unjustly." Qur'aan 2:275 - 281

Usury is what promotes speculation without finan-cial-foundation and destroys secure economic growth. As a point worthy of noting: In Islam, there is no such thing as one declaring 'bankruptcy and thereby escaping one's debt. Bankruptcy is a death-blow to sound economic development.

A critical problem in today's society is that most everyone lives beyond his/her means. Elimination of usury would permit nearly every working individual to obtain and afford all his/her needs and most wants. Why should one buy a one hundred thousand dollar home and be forced to pay a lending institution nearly a half million dollars over the course of twenty-five to thirty years? This is financial slavery! Insanity!

Relative to the economy, let me quote from The Message Publications book entitled *Commandments by God in The Quran* as compiled by Nazar Muhammad:

"The rich have become oblivious of the needs of the poorer society. The percentage of of have-nots is on the increase. In the United States, Mr. Reagan, the former President, had openly declared that the Federal Government could no longer fund the needs of poorer society. He left them to be looked after by the state governments who had got limited funds. The aid to poorer families is becoming less and less every day.

"The situation in America is being repeated in almost all other developed countries. The other day there was a news item that in London alone, one million people had no shelter over their heads and were living on streets. The rich passers-by see the misery around them, but the demands of their artificial needs are so exorbitant and pressing, that they do not find any spare funds to relieve the unfortunate situation of the have-nots.

"Sweden is a highly developed country, with 95% or more of its population doing extremely well in the so-called amenities of the modern world. And yet, surprisingly, all their luxury is fake. It fails to give these people true happiness. They seem to feel that they lack something of such a paramount importance that, without it, life is meaningless and futile. No wonder that the rate of suicide in Sweden surpasses all other countries.

"On the international level, sharp division has occurred in the so-called North and South countries. The sympathy that leaders of North express for the poor South is merely lip service. Although it is appreciated that there cannot be any lasting peace unless living standards of the South are raised, yet the developed countries have no funds either to write off the existing debts of the developing countries or to give them further loans for development.

"The loans to the poor nations had been mostly in the form of armaments which were priced very high with interest rates unpayable by the recipients of these loans. It will be well nigh impossible for them to pay the same. The developing countries have to pay a sum of 1,500 billion dollars! The amount being loaned to them these days is hardly sufficient for paying back the installment of the loans as well as interest. If the debtor countries adhere to payment on schedule, they have got hardly any funds for development of their economy and necessary social uplift of their people. The crisis might develop so that existing governments are overthrown and there is a general chaos. One can imagine the hazards to be faced by developing countries as well as developed countries.

"The aid that was granted to the poor countries was actually a loan with heavy interest rates. As they could not repay the same, the sum total that they owed to lenders has become so heavy that there is almost a refusal to pay back. Negotiations are being held to make repayments according to revised schedules, but there are very few Lenders who will forego the repayments.

"Same is the case with individuals. The condition of the debtor is rarely taken into view in a compassionate way. Everyone looks to his own rights, but nobody considers his obligations to help the poor in the real sense of the term.The economy as a whole has become unmanageable. If any intelligent being from outer space were to see what humans on this globe were doing to one another, he would hardly believe his eyes!

"In the 1960's or early 1970's, the university students in America and younger generation adopted hippyism. It meant that hippies disdained the present system of accumulating wealth. They decried the life of those who from morn till evening were busy accumulating what they considered as wealth. A scion of Kennedy tribe committed suicide about five years back. It was said to be an over-dose of some drug. The question arises, why should such a wealthy young man start taking drugs? The answer, perhaps, is that his own wealth and the wealth of his family did not prevent him from taking to drugs so that he could become oblivious of the ills of society.

"IN SHORT, THERE IS NO PEACE OF MIND TO BE FOUND ANYWHERE IN THIS WORLD. Industrial development is no answer."[1]

Now, what, we must ask ourselves, is the answer?

In exploring this question I must first direct our view to the religious communities of America. (Did not Jesus, God's peace be upon him, do battle with the money lenders?) How do we morally improve ourselves, provide continued upward stimulation to our economy and eliminate usury from our lives?

An answer can be found within the text of a khutbah (sermon) which I recently delivered at Virgin Islands International Islamic Society Mosque in St. Croix. Of that sermon, entitled "What Brotherhood Would Do For Us... If

83

We Had Some", I shall relate the following:

"Today I am going to step on your toes but I will try not to mess up your shine, because we are supposed to be brothers; but are we really? Besides being the best Da`wah (example) for non-Muslims, *brotherhood* (If we had some) would help us Muslims, socially, economically and spiritually. Today, by the mercy of Allah, I shall attempt to give you some realistic examples. Examples which if put into practice would, Insha'Allah, "....qoo-waa anfusakum wa ah-leekum naa-ran/wa qoo-duhaan-naasu wal-Hijaarah, ..." As All Mighty Allah commands of us to "..save yourselves and your families from a Fire whose fuel is men and stones..." A Fire which Allah personifies in Qur`aan to the effect that when the sinners are seen by it, from a place far away, the sinners will hear its fury and its raging sigh (of desire for them). "...sami`uu lahaa ta-ghay-yu-dhan wa za-fee-ra ....(zafeer).

"First, since we all love money, let us see what brotherhood (If we had some) could do for us economically. Let us take the issue of Insurance. We all have the need to purchase insurance every year, and we pay through the nose for it. The purpose of insurance is to be a safeguard against the dangers of losses which are consequences of human life and everyday dealings, and when such occasions occur, the individual is completely destroyed if the assistance of the community or his group is not available. The community as a whole can absorb such losses but the individual would be totally ruined if he has to carry the burden alone. The question is whether it is to be the actual loss or the chance of loss that is to be covered by insurance.

"Therefore, it is a serious question throughout the Muslim world as to whether or not Insurance is lawful in Islam. The Muslim community stands divided into three groups over this issue. Some jurists say it is permissible in all of its forms; some reject it in all its forms, and others say it is permissible in only some of its forms.

"Let us look at the origin of insurance. For the idea of insurance is uniquely and innermost connected with the group because man is a social being and needs the help of a society in order to satisfy his needs. In this setting, different concerns and relations develop which results in a social structure of inter-dependence.   In other words, group-life or community-life is where the idea of insurance begins.

"Clearly, at the start of civilization, early man was no more than an animal in search of food and shelter.   He would hunt between long periods of hunger. In a next stage of his development he would settle down upon and around open plains and begin to cultivate and store his food, but he still is not civilized until he becomes an inhabitant of an area which is owned with a commom law and which is regularly cultivated. Then he becomes a city-dweller. The word civilization comes from a latin word 'civis' which means 'city'. Inn Khaldun, the renown Arab historian and philospher, says: "It is man's desire for food that generates within him the impelling force towards civilization, which is his highest stage in social evolution."[2] In the initial social structure, the family organization is the root, and as it grows, its offshoots form into groups, tribes or clans in which they claim a common ancestor. Now develops the need for insurance.

"Let us now look at central Arabia; a desert land surrounded by the sea on three sides and the fertile regions of Africa and Mesopotamia on the other. The Arabs were adventurous, brave, hardy and war-like. They loved to raid and plunder other tribes, especially hostile ones. If we look carefully we shall see that Insurance was a necesary feature of their existence. We shall see that they then, and we today, need insurance. The desert with its lack of natural resources induced a 'wandering' type of Bedouin existence and made the people hardy and strong. They grouped themselves into families and therein lay their unity and strength.

"As stated, they loved to raid and plunder other tribes. They would steal cattle, camels, horses, women and children, (what ever), but they would spill as little blood as possible so a blood-feud would not result. The women and children would be ransomed back to the plundered tribe and the booty would be fairly divided by set rules, with the Shaykh getting the largest share. And when a tribe suffered a loss, all men shared in the loss and it was the Shaykh who contributed more to offset the losses of his tribe. The tribe functioned as with one mind; the loss to an individual member was looked upon as a loss to the whole tribe, and the tribe took steps to cover his loss. By another name this would be called 'insurance'.

"Its greatest expression is in payment of blood-money. For without the payment of blood-money, a blood feud would result which could serve to destroy both tribes. This payment became a custom in pre-Islamic Arabia. The Hedayah refers to it as "Ma`aqil", (the plural is "Ma`qula"), which signifies the blood-money payment. It is derived from the word "`aql".

"The Encyclopaedia of Islam says: "`Aqila is the name of a man's male relatives who according to the precept of religious law have to pay the penalty (the `aql) for him, when unintentionally he has caused the death of a Muslim."

"This order is based upon a verdict of the Prophet (PBUH). One day during a quarrel between two women of the Hudhail tribe, one of them, who was with child, was killed by the other with a stone, which hit her in the womb. When, soon after, the other woman also died, the Prophet

(PBUH) ordered that her kin (`aqila, or her aaSaba), in accordance with an old custom, had to pay the penalty to the relatives of the woman who had been killed.

"Initially in pre-Islamic days, the payment was ten (10) she-camels. However, Abdul-MuTTalib, paternal grand-father of the Prophet (PBUH), ransomed his young son Abdallah (the Prophet's father-to-be) from a vow which he had made, by the sacrifice of ten she-camels, but because he had to repeat the sacrifice ten times to be successful, one hundred she-camels came to be considered the value of one's life. (In Europe a similar payment was called "wergeld".)

"So we see that insurance is no more than mutual coverage of accidental loss, by a group who are subject to share similar dangers. The key word here is mutual, where-by the insured are also the insurers. Here we are talking about the division of loss and not the transfer of loss, which is capitalistic and usurious, thus forbidden.

"Now, after saying all of this: What would brother-hood do for us (If we had some)? Well, let us use a number and say that there are one thousand Muslim homes and business ventures in the Virgin Islands, all of which need insurance. Let us propose that an average three thousand dollar, one time disaster deposit is appropriated from each home, and five thousand is deposited for each business venture to be insured. This would give us an immediate eight million dollar fund. The chosen administrators of our mutual fund would invest this money as a mutual fund, which would increase according to its profit making potential.

"Just imagine the money which each party would save over the years! Then, when that original depositor went out of business or died, this money would be returned to him or his estate, theoretically, and his heirs would then re-insure the home or business. This is very simple. Once the fund has significantly increased, money could be loaned, interest free, to qualified parties. It is so simple. This is one of the many things which brotherhood could do for us (If we had some).

"But no, we are satisfied with our own, pre-societal family units wherein we practice "aaSabiya", which has been defined as unlimited and unconditional loyalty to one's own specific family group. Which our prophet (PBUH) has labled as a form of 'disbelief'."

Now, what I have related is just a portion of that particular sermon. I'm sure most of you noted that automobile coverage, which would greatly increase the monetary pool, was not included. Also, to better understand the one time distaster deposit payment: It is to be repeated only if and when one has an occurrence necessitating payment on one's behalf.

ES: Imam Abdallah, it seems that you are proposing that religious communities provide insurance and banking services for their constituents. Is that a correct analysis?

Imam: I believe that the religious communities are the first logical groupings to consider for this purpose. This is America, and American principles should over-ride predjudicial barriers, as was indicated in the last portion of the above sermon. Also, this economic feature would have a profoundly positive impact upon the overall religious community of our country, resulting in greater cohesiveness of the adherents of each faith. Necessarily, one's membership within his religious community would be more central to him when it depicts a tangible concern for his protection and well-being.

On the other hand, although I believe it should, I do not believe that the government is morally prepared to do this. Politicians talk church but do not practice it. This is all food for thought. May we eat of it. May its nutrients fuel our thoughts and our actions. May we become well. May we truly become Americans and be an example to the world. May the chips fall where they may, for when the dust settles, the earth and its inhabitants will be better off in the sight of man and in the sight of God.

Chapter 7
Education, Health Care, Legal/Medical Professions, Drugs And Gambling

ES: Imam Abdallah, As-salaamu 'alaykum.

Imam: Wa-'alaykumus-salaam wa rahmatullah.

ES: Imam, This is our seventh installment of our current series and we have been informed that you are close to winding it up. Since we have had many positive responses on past installments, what do you intend to be the focus of this installment?

Imam: Yes. Yes. Daily, we see and hear news of a proposed national healthcare program. Surely this is important, but clearly there are many oversights which will prevent its long-term success if implemented. We shall speak on these matters as well as the medical profession itself. Also, the legal profession, education, drugs (including TV) and gambling. Then I wish to conclude with an insight into the bottom line on what is the primary ailment of the U.S. of America and the world at large. I want to show through this insightful conclusion that those who have the conscience and the will can make the difference — if there are enough of them.

First: *the medical profession*, more explicitly, the doctors of this country. We all probably have seen educational television advertisements in which parents' vocational wishes for their children are addressed. I can vividly recall one such advertisement wherein the parent indicated a wish to have a doctor in the family. (I can understand this wish because I have a daughter who is a doctor and another who is entering medical school.) However, one might ask, "What is wrong with that?"

To this I shall say quite openly that there is a double sided coin to be observed — the moral side and the social side. Both must be honestly considered and addressed. On the moral side, most doctors appear to be godless in their concepts of duty to God and His creation. They seemingly take their skills as entirely their own doings, look upon themselves as gods, and give thanks and praise only to some of their medical forerunners.

On the social side, this society puts most doctors into serious hock in order for them to begin to practice their trade. Then, they in turn get theirs back, eventually, from the public. What is needed is a national financial control center (NFCC) for all doctors and doctoral services. This center would regulate the operations of its own regional units and be operated by medical and non-medical professionals.

This apparatus would regulate doctor salaries based upon current averages vis.a vis. medical category, skill, education and experience, and would pay each doctor accordingly. It would have on staff a contingent of "shoppers for medical services" such as shoppers employed by a store to check on its employees. Few doctors would willingly risk their licenses by misconduct. Also, except for cases of court-determined criminal conduct, this center would accept and absorb all doctor-related liabilities. (Not private hospital liabilities.) Doctors could not be sued for malpractice.

All fees for services would be paid to the center directly via their regional units. Hospitals and clinics would be paid via a predermined scale only for their incurred expenses such as care, goods, occupancy and use of special equipment too costly for others to develop and own. In this way all costs could be covered by a national healthcare program.

Healthcare is the right of all people in the country, not the privilege of a few. Any attempt to implement a cost-effective health care program without the means to control medical costs and paperwork is a false strategy designed to fail. Each graduate doctor would receive, free of charge, all necessary financial set-up assistance after internship from the NFCC.

The medical profession would still be a 'high income' group. Certainly each individual medical institution and individual doctor could also benefit from his or her respective individual or group research developments, literary activities, etc. The public would be protected and better served, and the medical professionals (doctors) would still be a high income group with greater public respect and confidence. Of course, this is only the idea outline. People much better acquainted with the intricacies of healthcare than I would put the puzzle together.

The legal profession: Without going into extraneous detail, similar restraints need be affixed to the legal profession. Lawyers have been called many vile names because they feed off of the misery of those who can least afford to pay. This is true of all lawyers whether African, Asian, European or Hispanic. Lawyers are out to put bread and butter on their tables. Altruistic motives are very, very few; if any.

In this Islamically considered low-esteemed profession, the system makes one attorney no better than another, regardless of his/her race or faith. It is his/her ability to interpret, re-interpret, twist and manipulate the secular law of the land in favor of his/her client.

If the truth be told (and I intend to tell what I know), nearly all lawyers with the exception of some Europeans are in a day-to-day struggle to survive. Most survive/prey primarily off of the meanest of our society. Most do not get the big contracts. Most do not work for the big firms. Most do not get the big settlements. Many of them appear to be no more than starving vultures in business suits who have families to feed and bills to pay like the rest of us. Those who get lucky and who are not a part of corporate America, in their desire to become so, oftimes must put their consciences in storage because it often comes down to how well one knows the law and can perform, bend, twist and cheat man's imperfect set of societal by-laws, and not what is clearly right or wrong. My wife is an attorney who has passed the bar and practiced in two states. The built-in depravity of the profession and her Islamic conscience has all but weaned her out of it. Praise be to Allah, she is in a position to select her cases.

Justice based upon law can only prevail when man is using God's Law. Man, being imperfect, will necessarily still make errors even when attempting to implement God's Law. Therefore just imagine the built-in injustice which he, in the name of law, enacts toward his fellow man, when he relies upon his own imperfect law; while he himself is full of negative attributes which only God's chosen way can eliminate from him, such as racism, personal subjective prejudices, etc.

ES: Imam Abdallah, concerning the legal profession, why have you called it an "Islamically considered low-esteem profession"? Also, is not it true that these people have spent many years in school being educated in their chosen field?

Imam: I will answer your first question by simply saying that it is Islamically unsound to charge people for advice.

Our readers' research into this area will further educate them. When their findings corroborate mine, I will then not be charged with stigmatizing many Muslims who have chosen secular law as their profession.

To your second question I openly claim that these people are taught by being trained to respond in a particular fashion, primarily by being good researchers. In fact, it is usually the legal secretaries and researchers who do the 'gut work' for the attorneys. However, by stating this, I am not denying the intelligence of the average attorney. Here we have classic examples of the system making (destroying) the man rather than the man making (improving) the system.

To your second question I also shall respond by pointing out that there is a real problem with the United States educational system. So, let us take a short sojourn into the educational arena.

At the beginning of this decade, it became common knowledge that the U.S. of A. was educationally behind nearly every other industrialized nation of the world in the area of mathematics and the sciences. Thus, under the administration of President George Bush, the New American Schools Development Corporation (NASDC) came into being as a private, non-partisan, non-profit corporation. Its program was called "America 2000." The idea was to develop a stategy for restructuring the American school system from top to bottom by setting up 'model schools'. Under the Clinton Administration it has become the "Goals 2000: Educate America Act." We hear too little about it. Mr. David T. Kearns, who was appointed by President Bush, is the man still responsible for administering this program. This is a good thing. Its time is long past due.

If another truism be told, it is the fact that far too many people go to college to become teachers simply because it is the easiest college choice to make. Consequently, we have few dedicated (altruistic, if you wish) teachers. The concept of teaching is in a rut.

Let me give an example: Look at how many students take a foreign language in grade school, high school and college only to leave school unable to converse on any level of proficiency? What is the purpose? What is being taught? Grammar! Years of grammar and no proficiency! Why not teach the Berlitz method or the Sybervision method? Or one of the many other operational methods of learning a language instead of continuing the drudgery of the past and present? What is the purpose?

This same argument goes for many of the courses taught today in American schools. It is time for a serious change. In each school district there should be a school for gifted children who want to learn. In each school district there ought to be a school to teach specific sciences and trades for children who want to learn. The other side of this coin says that there must be mandatory public employment for all who do not wish to further their education, as well as for the incarcerated.

Further, the government spends so much money per year per child for education. This money should be in a per child account which the parent or guardian can decide, if he/she so chooses, to spend in the school of choice. This alone would mandate many changes.

I could go on and on, however I believe the point is well taken. There is a serious need for serious change in America's school system. The system is outmoded. In the life of man, in his every endeavor, the controlling system need be reviewed, scrapped, revised or replaced if his performance is according to its dictates and yet he still finds himself failing.

Drugs and Gambling: To reiterate what has already been said in these pages concerning illegal drugs, no real prohibition of drugs can nor will take place in societies which legalize the worst drug of all, alcohol. It is absolute folly to legalize alcohol, the worst and most damaging drug of all, and then think that the same people who openly and freely use and abuse one drug (alcohol) are going to rid the country of any others. No intelligent person can realistically think so.

Also, Allah, The Most High, tells us thus in The Qur'aan concerning alcohol and gambling: "They ask you concerning wine and gambling. Say: `In them is great sin, and some profit, for men; but the sin is greater than the profit.' ...." Surah (chapter): 2, Ayat (sign/verse): 219

"Believers, wine and games of chance, idols and divining arrows, are abominations devised by the devil. Avoid them, so that you may prosper." Surah: 5, Ayat: 90

"The devil seeks to stir up enmity and hatred among you by means of wine and gambling, and to keep you from the remembrance of Allah and from your prayers. Will you not abstain from them?" Surah:5, Ayat:91

Gambling too is a form of addiction, like a drug addiction. To get a fuller view of this addiction for what it is, one needs only to look at the 'instant winner' lottery games promoted on television in many western states. The situation has become so onerous and openly damaging to the public interests in some of these states that some have introduced legislation to ban their TV promotion. People's lives are being utterly ruined by this TV promoted addiction.

It is worth noting that at the outset of this installment I listed television as a drug. While not mitigating the effects of alcohol, TV is perhaps the greatest drug of all. Television promotes the greatest across-the-board demoralizing effect upon society known to man. Television is hypnotic.

Television is the most dangerous tool in the immoral hands of those who control society. Without doubt, television provides man with his greatest moral test to overthrow evil and advance toward righteousness.

TV programming must be controlled. Like a weapon of any calibre, TV is only a tool. However, its power is in its innate addictiveness regardless of the programming; which is why many Islamic scholars have labeled TV as "haraam" (unlawful to own or watch).

However, in my humble and non-account opinion, there are many 'lawful' things which could be categorized as unlawful depending on the intent of their use. Grapes procured for the production of wine would be Islamically unlawful. What must be kept in mind is that 20th/21st century technology must never supplant 7th century morality.

CHAPTER 8
THE SOLUTION

ES: Imam Abdallah, As-salaamu 'alaykum.

Imam: Wa-'alaykumus-salaam wa rahmatullah.

ES: Imam Abdallah, you have covered many interesting topics during the course of this series. Now, in this concluding episode, what is to be your focus?

Imam: It surely was my intention to enlighten, inform and entertain. However, what I proposed was sincerely meant to be food for thought and a mental thrust toward initiating our conditioning process for change; a change for the better (Insha'Allah).

Just as an athlete, a student or anyone who is reaching for excellence must condition one's self for the test to come, we Americans must do the same if history is to record us coming out on top during these turbulent times. The subject of my focus shall be explaining the conditioning process.

ES: We must interject at this point to remind you that many African-Americans do not acknowledge themselves as "Americans."

Imam: Well, to that I ask, "Where are they planning on going?" We must be for real.

Nationalistically, the descendants of Africans who have been born generation after generation on these shores are American, by birthright. In or out of that context, they are Americans. The quality of life they live as American citizens of the future depends 100% upon themselves irrespective of and in spite of their past disenfranchisement. As the saying goes: "What have you done for yourselves lately?"

This aspect of who African-Americans are and have the right to be has been covered in depth during the series, and it is bitter medicine for many. I am not an idealist. The idealist must eventually succumb to reality, or he simply falls from the grace of his idealism because of his innate humanness. I see the world through the eyes of a theological pragmatist; ever willing to deal with the current reality according to God's dictates as I understand them; as an optimist ready to accept pessimistic realities.

As I have said many times before, "There is a political reality to every situation". This is real. Let us all, African/Asian/European-American, intelligently deal with the reality or succumb to it! Change is necessary for us all. Whether we like it or not, western society is dying right before our eyes, like a man with cigarette induced lung cancer who does not have the strength of will to stop smoking. Like the people of prohibition.

The Qur'aan shows us that earthly creation moves in time cycles; like the night giving way to the day, which is the only completed action which takes place overnight. And even then the day eventually succumbs to the night. This action proves that patience, which is often overlooked and under-acted, is the catch word in man's languages. Lack of patience results in an overwhelming desire for materialism.

The Prophet MuHammad (peace be upon him) is reported to have said that haste is from Satan. Let us look at the recent despicable state of affairs in the state of Florida where European tourists have been routinely murdered by young African-Americans. One African-American adult who was interviewed about it called these marauders and murderers "soul-less". And they are. They have become as conquered by Satan as any cruel European-American slave owner of the deep South.

Let us look at Bosnia vis-a-vis the United States Department of State, wherein mid-level administrators, those who do the work and know, severely criticize Warren Christopher et. al. and the U.S. State Department policy. A policy that stands idly by and watches a people being exterminated and at the same time ties their hands so they cannot defend themselves. All in the name of political expediency. (We might also note that a new center extolling the horrors of the the Jewish holocast has just been opened in Washington, D.C.; supposedly as a reminder to the world of its inaction at that time!)

The two scenarios contain the same type people. "Soul-less." This is the primary problem with the world. It is controlled by people who have lost their souls to The Devil. And, yes, they are being opposed, but primarily by people who have also lost or are daily losing their souls. The latter's desire is not for justice to prevail, they just want their "piece of the pie". There are just too few and too passive God-conscious people in the world today, when they are sorely needed.

What is the remedy? Is there one? I say yes. Always!

The remedy consists of first recognizing Satan for who and what he is, and to recognize and judge his exploits for what they are. Wherever man sees man's inhumanity to man, regardless of the surface issues, man must recognize it as the work of the Devil.

In order for man to see beyond the surface of any evil scene, he must cultivate the spiritual, higher qualities of his soul (if he believes he has one). In order for man to do this, he/she must necessarily understand the intrinsic qualities and realities of his/her soul.

"By the soul and the proportion and order given to it. And its enlightenment as to its wrong and right. Truly he succeeds who purifies it. And he fails who corrupts it!" Qur`aan 91: 7-10

The mind of man is governed by his soul, therefore, his intellect (which is a product of his mind) must be the parent guardian of his child-like soul ...because: "...men's souls are swayed by greed." Qur`aan 4:128  ...because: "the (human) soul is certainly prone to evil,..." Qur`an 12:53 ...because: "We (God) know what dark suggestions his soul makes to to him (man)..." Qur`aan 50:16

Soul may be considered related to conscience at one point in its development, and is what gives man his ability to think. His intelligence is what gives him his ability to reason. Soul goes through three stages of development which has already been explained in detail in these pages. We must all immediately and honestly assess the inner quality of our souls and work from there.

This assessment gives us our starting point. For example: when something goes wrong for you, whether it be a stubbed toe, a car accident, or any unexpected tragedy, what is your first response? Is your immediate response a curse word or a demeaning gesture? (Most people would have to give an unqualified "yes" to this question.) Or, do you remember God and give Him praise?

Do you think of your own impending death? Do you remember to think of it often? One who doesn't is said to be living in a fool's paradise. Our Prophet Muhammad (peace be upon him) admonished man to think of his death often, and is reported to have said, "If you could have seen what I see, you would weep much and laugh little."

Here we see four types of men:

(1) For the worldly man, death is greatly displeasing to him/her. He/she envisions death as a 'spoiler' and he/she therefore gives up all thoughts of it and fears its coming. He/she is an affirmed materialist and is quite a distance from his/her Lord and has already become impoverished thereby.

(2) The repentent person wants death to be delayed for the sake of being engaged in repentance and for the hope of crediting more good deeds to his/her account.

(3) The 'good person' who thinks he is ready to meet death because he believes in God and awaits his meeting with Him.

(4) The truly religious man who does not feel pleased nor displeased with his impending death. He is quite simply resigned to submit (willingly) to the will of Allah.

Man is the only subject in God`s creation which has been given soul. "And they ask you about the soul. Say: The soul is one of the commands of my Lord, and you are not given aught of knowledge but a little." Qur`aan 17:85

Soul is a divine thing and may be compared to a microcosm of God`s light. This is what makes man lord of creation. Soul is what gives man his special connection with God. "Then He (God) made him (man) complete and breathed into him of His spirit, and made for you the ears and the eyes and the hearts; little is it that you give thanks." Qur`aan 32:9

As already said, change is necessary for us all. For if change were not possible we would already be doomed. There would be no rationale for education, classes, lectures, sermons, etc. The Prophet said: "Make your conduct good." If change were not possible, this advice would have been of no value, useless. The necessary change is a change in soul. With the view toward protecting, changing, perfecting one's soul, I excerpt the following from Imam Ghazzali's Ihya

Ulum-id-Deen *The Revival Of Religious Learnings*:

"Know, dear readers, that soul is like a fortress and the Devil wishes to enter it and commit havoc. In order to save it from the Devil, one must guard the doors of this fort. It is impossible for him to guard them unless he knows the doors, which are his character and conduct.

(1) **Anger and sexual passion** is a great door for the Devil's entry. When intelligence is weak, the forces of the Devil attack it. It is related that Moses (peace be upon him) once interceded for the Devil and as a result the Devil gave Moses (peace be upon him) this advice: "One should remember me at the time of three things and I shall not do him any harm."

When he gets angry, he should remember that my life is with his soul, my eyes are with his eyes and I move within him like the circulation of his blood.

When one joins a fight, he should remember that I come down at that time and I remind him of his wives, children and properties, as a result he flees away.

One shall not sit by such a woman who can be married, I stay with her as his messenger. I don't stop til I make him fall in danger.

(2) **Hatred and greed** is another great door for the Devil to enter the soul. When a man has got greed for anything it makes him deaf and blind, as the Prophet (PBUH) has said. The Devil has said that he has been cursed with hatred and that he generated greed in Adam (PBUH) and misguided him.

(3) **Eating with satisfaction** (to one's heart content) is another door for the Devil as it makes the sexual passion strong (unmanageable). Eating to one's full creates six harms:
—God-fear goes out of the heart of such a person
—Kindness for the people goes out of one's heart
—One has difficulty in doing divine service
—One is not humble when one hears words of wisdom

—When he gives a sermon, it does not enter into the hearts
of the audience

—Many diseases grow in him.

(4) **Inordinate love for fine things** is another door for the
Devil.

(5) **Dependence on people** and to cherish hope for their
favors is another door for the Devil.

(6) **Hastiness** in action and to give up firmness in action
are another door of the Devil.

(7) **To possess wealth beyond necessity** is another great
door for the Devil. He who has got the necessities lives in
peace, but if one possesses surplus wealth, he cannot enjoy
peace as he wants more and more.

(8) **Miserliness** and fear of poverty, another great door, as
they prevent charity and expense, encourage hoarding and
create greed for wealth.

(9) **Staying in the streets** and markets. The Prophet
(PBUH) said: When the Devil came down to the Earth, he
said: O Lord, give me place for habitation. God said: I give
you bathroom/toilet-room for habitation. The Devil said; Give
me place for assembly. God said: For that I give you streets
and markets. The Devil said: Give me food. God said: You
are given food over which God's name is not mentioned. The
Devil said: Give me drink. God said: I give you drink which
produces intoxication. The Devil said: Give me an inviter.
God said: I give you instruments of song. The Devil said:
Give me a Qur'aan. God said: I give you poetry. The Devil
said: Give me a book. God said: I give you pictures of animals. The Devil said: Give me traditions. God said: I give you
false talk. The Devil said: Give me game: God said: I give
you women."

These nine points represent only some of the means
by which Shaytan/Satan destroys the souls of man.

EPILOG

The presentation herein is intended as an awakener to those God-conscious people who carry the mantle of responsibility as God's viceregents on earth. For certain, His Will will be done.

Man knows what corrupts him. He sees his social condition worsening by the day. He must summon the strength which he needs to fight a winning fight. This he cannot do without God's help because he is fighting against the forces of the Devil who is a many faceted being, a multi individual. The Devil is not always singular except as a general descriptive concept.

There are many devils. Some are spiritual in nature, some are physical. Their chief is known as Iblis, the wicked one, one who is without hope; Shaytan, the one who opposes and one who is far from the truth. This Chief Devil is singular and on Judgement Day will be destroyed by God. There is the Devil of Wicked Violence. There is the Devil of Drugs and Intoxicants. There is the Devil of Immorality. These three devils are at the root of the destruction of civilization, worldwide. It is said that lead destroyed ancient Rome. It has been said that sugar weakened the rule of Islam. I say that high-tech immorality and illegal drugs (including alcohol) far out-weigh violence in the on-going breakdown and impending destruction of American society.

We hear much about crime and violence. We see a plethora of no-sense gun control laws passing through Congress and state legislatures. We see various national crime bills passing as well. Each decade more billions upon billions of tax-payer dollars are thrown away in like manner. More and more police are hired. More and more prisons are built. Yet, year after year, life is continually, compoundedly worse. Our cities are literally dying right before our eyes as well as the rest of western civilization.

When will Americans wake up to the fact that they must change their lifestyles and their value systems? There is no moral code of decency which can be called American or western. The latter three devils mentioned have absolute control of American media. In such a high-tech age, only a fool would or could believe that everything perverse in the media would not spill over, nay, flood over into general society just as they they spill over into our dreams!

We have attempted to explicitly and honestly address all these matters in this series. It is our sincere hope, and our task to help America live up to her lofty ideals by setting forth herein the proposed guidelines for structuring a new society, a truly American society.

Man's history will surely record and judge America's success or failure in these matters. Final Judgement belongs to All Mighty Allah (God). For sure, He will!

"There is no soul but has a protector over it. Now let man think from what was he created! He is created from a drop emitted – Proceeding from between the backbone and the ribs: Surely God is able to bring him back (to life)! The day that (all) things secret will be tested, (man) will have no power and will have no helper." Qur'aan 86:4-10

CONCLUSION

Islam is the only "religion" which has successfully fought and actually defeated all forms of man's inhumanity to man, viz. personal arbitrary subjective prejudices, including racial intolerance. It offers categorical proof to humanity that it is truly God's choice for all men because it was sent as a universal message by a universal messenger.

Prior to Islam, "revealed religion" did not have a formal name. It was named after the particular Prophet of God who expounded upon the "faith" under God's direction, and was thus known as "The religion of Abraham", or "the religion of Moses", etc. Nor was God known by a formal name which could be spelled out and accurately pronounced, but only as the "God of Abraham", or "the God of Moses", etc.

Yet, all of the prophets taught one and the same message; submission to the will of God, Islam. With the end of the mission of Muhammad, who is the seal, the last of the prophets (peace be upon all of them), Allah/God said: "This day have I perfected your religion for you, completed my favor upon you, and have chosen for you Islam as your religion." Qur'aan 5:4

America has lofty ideals which are really based upon a Judeo/Christian ethic. This is no secret! These ethics are based upon the commands of God. Which is why we find some relative degree of success, although America's religious conscience fails so miserably when she should be achieving so much more! America needs a strong infusion of Orthodox Islam. More than any other group, Orthodox Muslims have the ability to morally stabilize this great country, the greater number being African-American; America's own. Orthodox Muslims represent the final and the missing piece of the puzzle to America's beautiful "patchwork society."

I believe that the attainment of America's lofty ideals are within her reach. She needs only an infusion of Islamic principles to bring them home to her bosom and into her heart. The inclusion of the Islamic principles espoused herein will surely fulfill her needs.

And Allah is The Best Knower.

GLOSSARY
of common Arabic terms used herein

Abdallah	servant/slave of Allah
abu	father
Al-Andalus	Arabic name for Islamic Spain
Allah	The One And Only True God of all created things, seen and unseen
Al-Haqq	The Truth
al-Hamdulilaah	The Praise (all of it) belongs to Allah alone
Al-Khaliq	The Creator
Amir	Prince, ruler, overall organizational leader
Arab	one who speaks the Arabic language
As-salaamu 'alaykum	The peace be upon you (said in the plural sense)
Ayah	a minor division of The Qur'aan, a verse
bayt	house
Baytul-Khaliq	House of The Creator
da`wah	generally meaning: propagation of the message of Islam
deen	the code of life ordained by Allah
Dhimmee	a non-Muslim permanent resident of a Muslim State who is automatically under the protection of the Muslim government
fiqh	Islamic jurisprudence
hadith	story, account, tradition of The Prophet Muhammad (PBUH)

ibn	son (placed in front of the name of the father); bin = son (as placed between the son's name and the father's)
Imam	Islamic title denoting leadership under the Amir's authority
iman	faith
insha'Allah	be it the will of Allah; If Allah so wills it to be
Islam	self-surrender to the will of Allah as was the example set by all of the prophets of God throughout known history
khalifah	viceregent (of God)
kufr	disbelief
maHr	free gift that husband gives to bride upon marriage
maHram	Muslim male so related to woman as to prohibit they marrying each other (Father, grandfather, uncle, brother, son, nephew)
majlis	an Islamic council
Masjid Baytul-Khaliq	
	a mosque name "House of the Creator"
masjid	formal Muslim house of ritualized worship
Maasha`Allah	"It is as Allah has willed or allowed
Moors	Africans who on several known occasions in the past 2000 years and before, invaded and conquered Spain, et al.
MuHammad	One who is highly praised, Name of the prophet of Islam
Muslim	One who willingly submits to the will of Allah

nastaghfirullah	May Allah forgive (protect) us
(PBUH)	Peace Be Upon Him (said after the name of any prophet of God)
Quraish	the Arabian tribe into which Prophet Muhammad was born
Qur'aan	literally, that which is to be read {The Book revealed to Prophet MuHammad, who was an illiterate prophet like unto Moses (PBUT)}
Shahadah	testimony, witness, etc. The Muslim creed doctrinal/formal
Shaykh	an elderly Muslim man; a Muslim leader or scholar
subHana wa ta`alaa	The Glorious and Most High (used for Allah only)
surah	a major division of The Qur'aan, a chapter
wa	and
wa `alaykumus-salaam	and peace be upon you (said in the plural sense)
wa raHmatullah	and The Mercy of Allah
wakeel	agent
wali	legal guardian
Yasin	(pronounced: Yaaseen) Mystical title of the 36th surah of Qur'aan and one of the one hundred attributes of Prophet Muhammad (PBUH)

NOTES

CHAPTER 1. HOW DO WE GET THERE FROM HERE?

1. Shaykh Abdullah Yusuf Ali, *Translation And Commentary Of The Holy Qur'aan*, Dar al Arabia Publishing, 1968 edition; surah/chapter 61 (Suratul-Saff/surah/chapter entitled: Battle Array), ayah/verse 9, page 1541.

2. Ivan Van Sertima, *Golden Age of the Moor*, compiled works, Transaction Publishers; New Brunswick, U.S.A., 1992.

3. Stanley Lane-Poole, *The Moors in Spain*, Publishers United, Ltd.; Lahore, Pakistan.

CHAPTER 2. CULTURE, NEIGHBORHOODS, SCHOOLS AND BUSINESSES

1. Dr. Jawanza Kunjufu, *Black Economics*; African Images, 1991.

CHAPTER 3. SPORTS, ENTERTAINMENT AND INTELLECTUALISM

1. Shaykh Abdullah Yusuf Ali, *Translation And Commentary Of The Holy Qur'aan*, Dar al Arabia Publishing, 1968 edition; surah/chapter 47 (surah/chapter entitled: MuHammad), ayah/verse 36 with accompanying notes, pages 1, 387 and 1388.

CHAPTER 4. MORAL RELATIONSHIPS—MARRIAGE AND SEX

1. The four (4) primary Orthodox Schools of Islamic Law are named after the four great men of exemplary Islamic repute. They are: Hanifi, Maaliki, Shaa'fi and Hanbali. In actuality they are only different branches of the same 'tree' of Islamic Thought. The same which has been endorsed by the Prophet MuHammad himself (PBUH) and is called Ahlus-Sunnah wal-Jamaa'ah (the people who keep to The Sunnah (prophetic traditions) and The Community (Companions of the Prophet)).

CHAPTER 5. CRIME AND PUNISHMENT

1. The Book Of Matthew, *Parallel-Column Edition Of The Holy Bible (containing the King James and the Revised Versions with complete concordance)*, F.F. Spyer and Company, 1880.

CHAPTER 6. BANKING, INTEREST, INSURANCE AND THE ECONOMY

1. Nazar MoHammad, *Commandments By God In The Qur'aan*, Message Publications, New York, First North American edition, 1991. (see forward, *The Economy*, p. xvi.).

2. Ibn Khaldun, *The Muqaddimah*, Vol. 1, p. 89 (translated from the Arabic by Franz Rosenthal).

BIBLIOGRAPHY
AND WORKS OF REFERENCE AND SUGGESTED READING

The author gives thanks and praise to Allah/The One and Only God for the following contributions:

Shaykh Abdullah Yusuf Ali, *Translation And Commentary Of The Holy Qur'aan*, Dar Al Arabia Publishing, 1968 edition

Shaykh Abul A`la Maududi, *The Meaning Of The Qur'aan*, Islamic Trust publications, Lahore Pakistan (English rendering by `Abdul-`Aziz Kamal, M.A.)

Ivan Van Sertima, *Golden Age Of The Moor*, compiled works, Transaction Publishers; New Brunswick, U.S.A., 1992

Anwar AHmad Qadry, *Islamic Jurisprudence In The Modern World*, second edition, 1973, Sh. MuHammad Ashraf Publications; Lahore, Pakistan

The Book Of Matthew, *Parallel-Column Edition Of The Holy Bible (containing the King James and the Revised Versions with complete concordance)*, F.F. Spyer and Company, 1880

Stanley Lane-Poole, *The Moors In Spain*, Publishers United, Ltd.; Lahore, Pakistan

Henry Copée, *History Of The Conquest Of Spain By The Arab-Moors*, Brown and Company; Boston, Massachusetts, 1881

Charles Hamilton's translation of *Commentary On The Islamic Law, The Hedaya (The Guidance)*, Islamic Book Trust, 1980

Nazar MuHammad, *Commandments By God In The Qur'aan*, Message Publications, 1991

Dr. MoHammad Muslehuddin, *Insurance and Islamic Law*, Islamic Publications, Ltd.; Lahore, Pakistan, 1969

Imam Al-Ghazzali, *Ihya Ulum-id-Deen (The Revival Of Religious Learnings)*, 1971 first English edition; F.K. Islamic Mission Publishers; East Pakistan

Masjid Baytul-Khaliq, Inc., *Shahadah Educational Journal*; Volume 6, Numbers 5 and 6, 1992; Volume 7, Numbers 1 through 6, 1993 Newark Community Masjid; Newark, New Jersey